Stuck!

Stuck!

Stuck!

Learn to Love Your
Screenplay Again

Josh Miller

19 20 21 22 23 5 4 3 2 1

Brush Education Inc.
www.brusheducation.ca
contact@brusheducation.ca

Cover design: Dean Pickup
Cover image: Charlieaja/Dreamstime.com
Interior design: Carol Dragich, Dragich Design

Printed and manufactured in Canada

Library and Archives Canada Cataloguing in Publication

Title: Stuck! : learn to love your screenplay again / Josh Miller.

Names: Miller, Josh, author.

Identifiers: Canadiana (print) 2018906675X | Canadiana (ebook) 20189066768 | ISBN 9781550597837

(softcover) | ISBN 9781550597844 (PDF) | ISBN 9781550597851 (Kindle) | ISBN 9781550597868 (EPUB)

Subjects: LCSH: Motion picture authorship—Handbooks, manuals, etc.

Classification: LCC PN1996 .M55 2019 | DDC 808.2/3—dc23

We acknowledge the support of the Government of Canada
Nous reconnaissons l'appui du gouvernement du Canada | Canadä

To my wife Michele
(I'm so glad I accepted that invitation)

Contents

Author's Note

Throughout this book, I cite examples from popular movies to illustrate screenwriting concepts. With so many decades of film from which to choose, it made sense to aggregate the titles into two groups based on the year they were made.

So for our purposes, "classic" films are those made prior to the year 2000 and "contemporary" films are those made since the year 2000. A list of all the films from which I've drawn examples can be found in Appendix I.

When I teach my classes, I find that referencing film examples really helps to illuminate all the concepts. So if there are movies listed in Appendix I that you haven't seen—or haven't seen in a while—I recommend screening them in tandem with this book.

Preface

Imagine for a moment that I'm the ShamWow or OxiClean Guy:

> "Folks, has this ever happened to you? You get a great idea for a screenplay, you sit down to write it, then about thirty pages in, you're lost. You take a few more stabs at it, but can't solve the story, so you shove it in a drawer, never to be seen again...."

OR, the alternate version:

> "...you get to the end of the script, leave it for a couple of weeks, then read it over and your heart sinks because the script is pure, unadulterated crap, and you don't know how to fix it. So you shove it in a drawer, never to be seen again...."

OR, the alternate alternate version:

> "...you get to the end of the script, give it to a few family members and colleagues to read, and they offer you 'encouragement' through tight smiles. You suspect the script is pure, unadulterated crap. So you shove it in a drawer, never to be seen again...."

OR, the alternate alternate alternate version:

> "...depressed by any or all of these outcomes, you don't write anything."

AND, inevitably, the come-on:

> "Well, folks...have I got a product for you!" [hard sell ensues]

Okay, so I'm not the ShamWow or OxiClean guy, and I'm not going to put a hard sell on you. But if while reading any of the above scenarios you nodded or winced from the memory of your own failed screenwriting efforts, then this book may be for you.

I'll elaborate. Let's say you like music. Perhaps you're an expert in music appreciation. Maybe you can even sing a bit and/or play some chords on a guitar. One day you hear a lousy piece of music on the radio and you say to yourself, "I could do better than that."

So you sit down to write a better piece of music. You may have some great musical ideas, but you know nothing about composition, arrangement, rhythm, melody, mode, and so forth. All this is woefully apparent in your completed piece, which…sucks.

Few among us would believe we'd be able to compose complex music with no formal training and no experience. And yet, inexplicably, a lot of dabblers think they can write a screenplay without any training or experience. It usually goes something like this:

> You have a great idea. Maybe even a fantastic idea. And because you read books or you've edited newsletters or maybe you wrote a play

that was staged by your community theatre, you
think: "I could write a screenplay!" But inevitably
one of the above depressing scenarios is the
outcome. Dreams are dashed. Your day job looms
large.

It doesn't have to be that way. I can show you a path through
the script wilderness. In addition to having a successful career
as a film and television writer/producer, I've taught scores of
emerging writers of all ages and backgrounds the concepts in
this book. I've also been honored to receive a Writers Guild of
Canada award for mentoring writers.

I'll show you time-tested techniques that will help you to
identify what your story is *about* so that you'll be able to invent
and employ elements in your narrative that are organic, while
discarding elements that are inorganic.

An **organic** element is one that fits naturally and easily in
your story and/or genre, that is, it "belongs." Inorganic elements seem forced or contrived and evoke a "what's wrong
with this picture?" feeling, as they'll stick out in an obvious
way. Sound complicated? It's not.

You'll learn how to avoid heading down **blind alleys** or
including extraneous characters or allowing your narrative
to wander, or worse, come to a dead stop in the middle of the
story. No longer will you get mired in the undergrowth and
abandon your journey.

I'm going to show you how to create a taut story from start
to finish that, in addition to being entertaining, will have a
point. And the message it will convey will be something that
for you will be authentic and deeply held. Above all, audiences
will be moved.

Creative endeavors always involve risk. But risk can be mitigated through knowledge. So if you're ready to take another shot at it and want to avoid repeating any of the above soul-crushing scenarios, you've taken the first step by seeking out this book.

Introduction

We're living in interesting times. People can not only access movies on multiple platforms, they can also film and edit their own low-budget films or programs and make their work available for global audiences via the Internet (for better or worse).

Movie theaters are doing business, but must compete for eyeballs by amping up the experience with digital projection, multichannel surround sound, large format screens, and 3D technology. Many are offering reclining chairs and seat-side food service.

Other exhibitors are niche programming their theaters with foreign and art house films or live events such as operas and music concerts. This is a positive development, I think, as it expands the demographic of those who go out to the cinema beyond just teenagers.

Youth still rules, however, and the Hollywood studios know that the surefire path to profit is to make comic book movies with awesome graphics, violence, gore, and mayhem. None of this is new, but it seems like it's gone to a whole other level.

These movies leave us feeling like we do after the large bag of popcorn we pound down while watching them—bloated and thirsty—and not just physically. Averse to empty calories, most of us consciously or unconsciously wish our movies were more nourishing.

Here's the thing: movies that nourish don't have to abandon flavor (entertainment value) for **substance**. Both can co-exist, and in fact I would argue that movies *with* substance are more entertaining and satisfying (while still commercial) than movies that lack substance.

What *is* substance? It's a **story** with a **point of view** held by the writer. The story itself is a vehicle the writer employs to prove his or her point. Not didactically, of course, because people don't want to be preached to outside of their church, temple, or mosque.

It's the telling of the story and its outcome that proves the writer's point, whatever it may be. The writer doesn't need to harbor a deep message; they just need something they firmly believe—it could even be contrarian—and a desire to share it with others.

Even young filmgoers who habitually attend **blockbuster** comic book films are so starved for substance that when they hear about an independent film with an original voice and an unambiguous point of view, they seek and devour it like manna from heaven.

An example like *Napoleon Dynamite* comes to mind, which of course is a classic underdog story, as are *Slumdog Millionaire* and *Little Miss Sunshine*. There's also *My Big Fat Greek Wedding*, a romantic **comedy** with an ethnic twist and *Juno*, a coming-of-age teen comedy. More recently, *Get Out* had a unique racial take on the psychological thriller genre. Note that none of these films featured huge movie stars or eye-popping special effects, yet all of them had a great story, well told, by fresh and appealing voices.

Right now you may be wondering, "What point of view do I have that I want to share with others?" Or perhaps you're thinking, "I just have a cool idea for a high concept movie with awesome characters and **dialogue**. I have no idea what I want to *say*."

If so, no worries. It's common to be unaware of your message at the outset of writing your story. It's not that you don't have deeply held beliefs; it's just that they have yet to be fully revealed. But they will. I'll show you how to do it. That's why I wrote this book.

Which brings us to a remarkable benefit of writing. Of course we want to tell stories and of course we want to entertain and enlighten audiences with our work. These things are a given. But in the process, we also gain something quite priceless. We learn who we are.

How to Use This Book

Stuck! is aimed at both emerging and veteran screenwriters. Emerging screenwriters will be exposed to concepts and techniques that will help them transform random and diffuse ideas into spare, taut narratives designed to move and enlighten.

Veteran screenwriters—like good doctors who are always scanning medical literature to stay current—will find concepts here that will add to their store of practical knowledge and will contribute to further elevating their work, taking their career to the next level.

Whether you've had work previously produced or have several screenplays "in the drawer," or whether you're contemplating getting into screenwriting for the first time, for most people, "learning by doing" often results in greater retention.

So if you're not a screenwriter but a story analyst or producer looking to hone your screenplay analysis skills, then consider applying the concepts in this book by writing mock coverage based on a few of the films listed in Appendix I.

If you're an emerging or veteran screenwriter, upon completing the chapters dedicated to specific aspects of screenwriting craft, consider challenging yourself to write one- to three-page scenes that incorporate what you've just learned.

If you're a member of a screenwriting group, you and your colleagues can read your scenes aloud and jointly **critique** them. I've used this technique during my classes and find that it adds an extra dimension to the learning process.

So whether for you getting "unstuck" means starting something new or reviving a half-completed work, armed with your new knowledge, you're going to have an "aha!" moment where you break through the muck and mire. Hopefully more than one.

Why am I so confident about this? Because I've seen it happen countless times with my students and with screenwriters with whom I've story consulted. It's like all the tumblers in a lock suddenly fall into place, opening a door to new and dazzling story riches.

The combination lies within.

The Kernel of the Idea

We're going to kick things off by spending what perhaps might seem like an inordinate amount of time looking at the source of story ideas. Why? Because it really helps to clear away a bunch of the weeds if you can articulate the source of your inspiration.

By that I mean the more you can categorize or classify your story, the easier it is to identify its genre along with its attendant conventions and, in so doing, avoid duplication, derivation or triteness (we'll go into much more detail on this stuff later).

And finally, it also helps to know what has come before in terms of similarly sourced stories, so you can watch and learn how they treated their subject matter. Sometimes the learning comes from seeing what *not* to do from unsuccessful movies.

Screen pundits pontificate that ideas are "a dime a dozen." What they're saying is that writing is all about the execution, and I completely concur. Nevertheless, one can't start writing anything without an idea, preferably one with some originality.

On that latter point, you've probably heard that there are only twelve basic plots. Or maybe nine. Or fifteen. Whatever the number, the notion suggests that every story has been told already many times over, so what can you contribute to the canon?

Yourself. No two people will tell the same story the same way. Your life experience and your voice, authentically shared, will ensure your material is original. Write what you believe and feel, not what you think others might want to read or screen.

Avoiding clichés is another tool in the kit, but we'll get into that in more detail later. Right now, we're addressing what I call the "**kernel**," meaning, simply, the germ of your story idea. The thing that got you going. The thing that first got you excited.

Here's the good news about kernels: they can be anything and come from anywhere. There's no correct or appropriate source for ideas. Inspiration knows no boundaries. So don't ever think your idea is unworthy because of its humble or obscure origins.

I would quickly provide one caveat, and that is when you're dogging a trend. By that I mean you've noticed that a certain genre or type of film seems to be in vogue, so you conceive or develop a similar idea with the intention of mining the same vein of ore.

Don't do it. Why? Because those movies were green-lit two or three years prior, and by the time you detect any sort of trend, it will already be passé, as trends by their nature are fleeting. Decision-makers will have already moved on to the "next big thing."

The other reason to forgo an "industrial" approach is that you likely won't follow through, either abandoning the screenplay or not starting it at all. Or if you do manage to complete a draft, it likely will be uninspired. The reason: you didn't really care about it.

Which brings us to the "P word": passion. I know you hear this word so often that you want to vomit, but the fact is, if you're not passionate about your idea, you're doomed. In the dark times—and trust me there will be dark times—nothing else will sustain you.

Without passion for your idea, you'll fold at the first negative critique. Usually that first negative critique will be your own. The only thing that will enable you to push through is *belief.* You may not yet believe in yourself as a writer (emphasis: *yet*), but you must believe in your idea. Only then will the kernel have a chance to sprout and grow.

Based on the notion that ideas can come from anywhere, in this section we're going to look at common sources of inspiration, illustrated by examples from contemporary and classic movies. Specifically, we'll look at character, situation, arena, genre, and adaptation.

Whether you're initially inspired to write about a particular situation or in a specific genre, or you decide to adapt an existing work or true story, ultimately your characters will drive the story, so we're going to spend a bit more time on them than the others.

Character

One great place to start is to create a character, either imagined or based on a real person, or some combination of both. First, ask yourself these questions:

1. What is it about this character that fascinates me?
2. Why do I think a story about this character will captivate others?

You'll note that I'm talking about a person, singular, not a group. With very few exceptions, stories are driven by a single central character known as the **protagonist**. The protagonist has also been called the "hero," but this might be a misnomer in stories where they're unlikeable. Or evil. Or tragic. So let's stick with protagonist.

While there are plenty of examples of **ensemble** films with multiple story lines and/or **central characters** that seem to be given equal weight, I suggest that upon closer analysis, these films actually provide a slightly greater focus on one of the story lines and its protagonist. Or alternatively, within each story line there's one clear protagonist.

We'll delve deeper into the role of the protagonist in chapter 4. For now, let's just consider protagonists as characters that are so interesting you want to fashion a story around them. I intentionally use the word "interesting" because we don't actually have to *like* them; we just have to give a damn about them, that is, be *interested* in their plight.

Think about that for a moment. "Caring" about them doesn't mean "liking" them. Of course it *could* include liking them, but at the end of the day, liking them isn't actually necessary or important. Being *interested* in them is the only thing that matters.

So what makes a character inherently interesting? Let's take a look.

Characters with contradictions

These types of characters immediately pique our interest because we know that two incompatible traits ultimately cannot co-exist in the same person. We know something will have to give and, like a slow motion car wreck, we're compelled to watch.

FILM EXAMPLES OF

CHARACTERS WITH CONTRADICTIONS

CONTEMPORARY FILM

Matchstick Men

Roy Waller (Nicolas Cage) is a con man with OCD, rendering him a neat freak who's afflicted with facial and vocal tics whenever he's under stress. When he learns he may have fathered a preteen daughter (Alison Lohman) and then meets her, his symptoms worsen as he soon finds himself caught between his "work" and his responsibility as a parent. These two worlds are bound to collide and the outcome is both unexpected and inevitable.

CLASSIC FILMS

Good Will Hunting

Will Hunting (Matt Damon) is a genius who's squandering his brilliance. We question why anyone who has such natural gifts would willingly forgo them. It makes us wonder whether there's been a traumatic event in his life and we're curious to learn what happened. We want to know whether his problems will be resolved and at what emotional cost.

Jerry Maguire

An agent with a heart. That's almost all one needs to say. Of course it's unfair to characterize agents as heartless, yet that's the perception. The notion that Jerry Maguire (Tom Cruise) is trying to become a better person is fundamentally at odds with the demands of his line of work. We know that this character is going to arrive at a crisis point and something is going to have to give, one way or the other.

Rebel characters

It's in these characters' DNA to defy convention and/or rise up against authority. While audience identification is key for any protagonist, rebels mine it in spades. It's not that most of us are rebels; it's that most of us *wish* we were rebels. We wish we exposed misdeeds, or stood up against injustice, or refused to accept the status quo when we know it's corrupt or immoral. Because of this, we admire and root for those who do.

FILM EXAMPLES OF
REBEL CHARACTERS

CLASSIC AND CONTEMPORARY FILMS

Dead Poets Society, V for Vendetta

Repressive societies are a staple of films that feature rebels. *Dead Poets Society* is a contained story at the quiet end of the spectrum, while at the loud end of the spectrum are films with scenes of societal revolution, such as *V for Vendetta*. A convention of the genre is that the protagonist may be sacrificed in the struggle, but they inspire protégés to take up the cause. John Keating (Robin Williams) inspires his students to take a stand and revolt against the reactionary prep school administrators, but it costs him his job. V (Hugo Weaving) dies fighting the forces of repression, leaving Evey (Natalie Portman) to carry out his explosive plot to topple the fascist regime.

The Fifth Estate, The Insider

Adding to the pantheon of rebels, a subcategory has evolved that could be described as "whistle-blowers," which would include Julian Assange (Benedict Cumberbatch) in *The Fifth Estate* and Jeffrey Wigand (Russell Crowe) in *The Insider*. These characters are controversial and often not widely beloved; nevertheless, when they reveal corporate or government secrets—an action they believe to be in the public interest—they risk everything, including their lives.

CONTEMPORARY FILM

Good Night and Good Luck

Defying their own TV network executives and sponsors, CBS news anchor Edward Murrow (David Strathairn) and producer Fred Friendly (George Clooney) take on Senator Joseph McCarthy, a red-baiting opportunist who's been alleging that communist sympathizers have infiltrated Hollywood, resulting in a blacklist. Murrow and Friendly put their jobs on the line and ultimately prevail when McCarthy is censured by the Senate and roundly discredited.

CLASSIC FILMS

One Flew Over the Cuckoo's Nest

In the inhumane milieu of a 1960s mental institution, our rebel character seems to be the only sane person in the joint. R. P. McMurphy (Jack Nicholson) is a libidinous, independent spirit, and because of the threat his freethinking presents to his minders, he's lobotomized. Do you recall the ending? It's another example of a rebel character inspiring a protégé.

Papillion

Henri "Papillion" Charriere (Steve McQueen) refuses to remain incarcerated, escaping from Devil's Island over and over again. In an unjust system, rebel characters will risk everything for freedom. Unbowed by authority, they're prepared to suffer any consequence, including death, because they know that the moment they cease to resist, they cease to be free.

Characters with nothing to lose

These are fascinating characters to write, because those who have nothing to lose are *capable of anything*. This freedom of action has great appeal for audiences, whose behavior is constrained by societal mores. You'll note that desperation and risk-taking are common features of these stories.

FILM EXAMPLES OF

CHARACTERS WITH NOTHING TO LOSE

CONTEMPORARY FILM

The Bucket List

This underrated film directed by Rob Reiner features Edward (Jack Nicholson) and Carter (Morgan Freeman), two elderly patients who meet in a cancer ward. In temporary remission, they create a "bucket list" of things to do together before they die. The film could have been a shticky senior citizen romp, but it's so much more because we learn that checking items off the list is not the end itself, but rather a means to a much more important end.

CLASSIC FILMS

The Full Monty

Here's a group of middle-aged blokes who can't buy a job. They become so desperate that they decide the only thing *less* humiliating is to become male strippers. Imagine the skill it takes to write a story in which a man taking off his clothes in public is an act that makes his young son proud, which we all find heartwarming! Now *that's* writing.

Going in Style

Three senior citizens (George Burns, Art Carney, and Lee Strasberg) are living a life of excruciating boredom. They decide to rob a bank, figuring the worst that could happen is that they'll get caught and live out their lives in jail, where they'll get three square meals a day.

Instead of getting caught, they go to Las Vegas and triple their loot. While the ending is bittersweet, it's fair to say that in the time they have left, they live life to the fullest.

Eccentric characters

Eccentric characters seem daft. They're oddballs who in life are easily dismissed; however, it turns out they have plenty to offer. We embrace these characters because we quietly relate; we all have our own idiosyncrasies for which we are judged, yet we too believe we have a lot more to offer than others perhaps give us credit for.

Eccentric characters have often experienced horrendous events in their past. These life experiences have given them insight and so as they deal with their own issues, the characters can also be **transformational**, meaning they can catalyze change in others.

FILM EXAMPLES OF
ECCENTRIC CHARACTERS

CONTEMPORARY FILM

Big Fish

Edward Bloom (Albert Finney) has always told implausible tales about his life. Now on his deathbed, his estranged son William (Billy Crudup) returns to get Edward to tell the truth. Edward recounts his life story, which is populated with bizarre characters. William slowly comes to understand that despite Edward's fantasies, his father has been a kind man. At Edward's funeral, William notices that many of the mourners bear a striking resemblance to characters in Edward's tales, although somewhat less exaggerated. Seeing that his father was only prone to embellishment, William decides to pass the stories down to his children.

CLASSIC FILMS

Being There

Chance (Peter Sellers) was raised by a rich man's housekeeper and never strays beyond the garden of their mansion, experiencing the world solely via television. When the old man dies and the mansion is sold, Chance is evicted and left to fend for himself. He's mistaken for a wealthy businessman and befriended by Eve Rand (Shirley MacLaine), wife of billionaire Benjamin Rand (Melvyn Douglas). Chance's naïveté is misinterpreted as homespun wisdom, and almost inconceivably, he becomes an advisor to the president of the United States.

The Big Lebowski

The protagonist in this quirky movie has become an icon. Even though the Dude (Jeff Bridges) is a confirmed slacker with a proclivity for drinking White Russians while being stalked by metrosexual Germans, he's an island of sanity compared to everyone else in the film. Despite his dysfunction, the Dude still has a moral compass, which we admire.

Harold and Maude

This poignant and bittersweet story delves into the friendship that develops between an unloved and lonely rich teen (Bud Cort), who repeatedly fakes suicide as an attention-getting strategy, and an elderly iconoclast (Ruth Gordon), who lives in an airstream trailer, poses nude as an artist's model, and attends strangers' funerals for fun. Intrigued?

Inspirational characters

These films feature people with physical or mental disabilities who find a way to overachieve. These stories inspire us, because as we watch them we quietly think, "If someone with these challenges can do these things, then I have no excuse." So true.

FILM EXAMPLES OF
INSPIRATIONAL CHARACTERS

CONTEMPORARY FILMS

The King's Speech

King George VI (Colin Firth) has a terrible stammer that's humiliating whenever he has to make a public speech. He finally agrees to undergo treatment with speech therapist Lionel Logue (Geoffrey Rush), who behaves like a cheeky commoner. The two men initially butt heads, but during the course of the speech therapy, they become friends. At the onset of World War II, George must address his country on radio with an inspirational message. With Logue's support, he doggedly nails the speech and shows he has the mettle to be a leader.

The Theory of Everything

Physicist Stephen Hawking (Eddie Redmayne) is stricken with ALS and given two years to live. Despite the diagnosis, he and his wife Jane (Felicity Jones) are determined to live a normal life for as long as possible. Hawking fathers three children and becomes renowned for his theories about time and space. Unfortunately, his marriage cannot withstand his illness, but he finds a new companion when he marries his nurse. Miraculously reaching old age, he reflects on his life and says his greatest achievement is not his work, but his children.

CLASSIC FILMS

Awakenings, Charly

Awakenings focuses on the relationship between Leonard Lowe (Robert Di Niro), a patient with a sleeping sickness, and his physician, Dr. Malcolm Sayer (Robin Williams), who awakens Lowe with an experimental drug that, alas, provides only a temporary cure. Inspired by his patient, Sayer realizes he's been hiding from life and decides to face his fears. *Charly* tells a similar story in which Charly Gordon (Cliff Robertson), a janitor with a low IQ, is given an experimental drug that turns him into a genius, only to have it slowly lose effect. His intelligence fading, he's tragically unable to prevent his intellectual regression.

Forrest Gump

Forrest Gump (Tom Hanks) has a low IQ, yet he consistently does one outstanding thing throughout his life: he keeps his word. Because of this, he has amazing exploits and achieves remarkable goals. Through him we learn that possessing integrity and character (i.e., doing the right thing and not the easy thing) trumps intellect every time.

Fish-out-of-water characters

These characters are innocent or naïve or don't understand the culture they've been parachuted into, and so at first they're marginalized, but they slowly show they have something unique to offer. They ultimately gain acceptance, despite their uniqueness.

FILM EXAMPLES OF

FISH-OUT-OF-WATER CHARACTERS

CONTEMPORARY FILMS

Elf

Buddy (Will Ferrell), a human raised by Santa and the elves at the North Pole, travels to New York to find his birth father, Walter Hobbs (James Caan). A DNA test confirms that Buddy is his son, so Walter takes him home and his wife Emily (Mary Steenburgen) insists they take him in. After many shenanigans due to Buddy's innocence, in the end, he helps revive the Christmas spirit and power Santa's sleigh while also getting Walter's business back on track.

Legally Blonde

Debutante and fashion merchandising major Elle Woods (Reese Witherspoon) is dumped by her boyfriend, who will be attending Harvard Law School. She decides to study hard and get admitted to Harvard in the hope that she can win him back. At Harvard, she's ridiculed for being shallow and clearly doesn't fit it with the intellectuals. Elle decides to get involved in a murder case, which she wins. With her star on the rise, her boyfriend now wants to reconcile, but Elle's no longer interested. She graduates with honors and is chosen class valedictorian.

CLASSIC FILMS

Big

Thirteen-year-old Josh Baskin wants to be a grownup. After he makes this wish to Zoltar, a fortune-telling machine, the next day he wakes up an adult (Tom Hanks). Chased out of his home, he ends up in a toy store, where he meets the CEO of a toy company (Robert Loggia). Recognizing his child-like qualities, the CEO hires Josh, who becomes incredibly successful. He meets Susan (Elizabeth Perkins), a cynical executive who falls in love with him, smitten by his honesty. However, she eventually realizes that he is really just a homesick boy and helps him go back. While saddened to lose him, she's grateful that he awakened her zest for life.

Coming to America

Akeem Joffer (Eddie Murphy), crown prince of the African nation of Zamunda, decides he wants to go incognito and find a wife in America who won't want him for his riches and high social status. Despite not knowing the ropes, he meets Lisa (Shari Headley) and they develop a romantic relationship, but then she learns that he's a royal. Angry that he lied to her, she breaks it off and he returns home, resigned to marry a woman who has been arranged for him. However, when he raises her veil on the altar, it's Lisa, who's had a change of heart.

Characters who "go native"

These characters reject their own culture or modern society for the promise of a simpler life, usually among an indigenous, less technologically advanced society. For these characters, there's more purity in embracing old ways or living close to the land, in harmony with nature.

The society they reject is usually colonial or imperialistic and has designs on the resources and land of the indigenous people. Often the protagonist bounces between both societies, leading to an identity crisis, but in the end they remain with their adopted people (or die trying).

FILM EXAMPLES OF
CHARACTERS WHO "GO NATIVE"

CONTEMPORARY FILMS

Avatar

Set in the future, soldier Jake Sully (Sam Worthington) is sent to infiltrate the Na'vi, an indigenous society on the planet Pandora. The military has been ordered to relocate the Na'vi in order to facilitate the mining of a valuable mineral. Sully is a paraplegic; however, he has full mobility when he inhabits his Na'vi avatar. It's not long before he falls in love with Neytiri (Zoe Saldana) and embraces the Na'vi ways, turning against his avaricious superiors.

District 9

Wikus Van De Merwe (Sharito Copley) is a white collar warrior who's tasked with forcibly relocating the Prawns, a race of ragtag aliens who have sought sanctuary on Earth. However, when Wikus is infected by a foreign substance and slowly begins to metamorphose into an alien, he's targeted for vivisection by the government. Wikus escapes and, now a fugitive, switches sides and helps a group of aliens return to the safety of their mothership, hoping they'll return in three years with a cure for him. In the end, we believe Wikus perished during a battle with government forces, but then we see a wounded alien fashioning makeshift gifts and quietly leaving them on the doorstep for Wikus's widow.

The Last Samurai

In 1876, US Army captain and Civil War veteran Nathan Algren (Tom Cruise), a disillusioned alcoholic, is hired to train the Imperial Japanese Army. Captured in battle by the samurai, he's taken to their village and as he learns their ways, he decides that he's been fighting for the wrong side. He overcomes his alcoholism, helps the samurai battle the Imperial Army, influences the emperor to act honorably, and retires to the samurai village to live out his life in peace with a Japanese woman and her children.

CLASSIC FILMS

Dances with Wolves
Following the American Civil War, suicidal Lieutenant John Dunbar (Kevin Costner) requests a posting on the Western frontier so he can see it before it disappears. He encounters the Pawnee, a Sioux community, who show him their ways. He marries Stands with a Fist (Mary McDonnell) but then has to leave the community because he's been deemed an army deserter and his presence endangers them. Not long afterward, however, the Sioux are subjugated by the American government, capping the conquest of the Western frontier.

Lawrence of Arabia
In 1916, T. E. Lawrence (Peter O'Toole), a colonel in the British Army, convinces feuding Arab tribes to fight against Ottoman Turkish rule in Sinai and Palestine. Lawrence exchanges his British uniform for Arabian robes and, with delusions of grandeur, he leads the Arabs into battle. In the end, he's unable to achieve his goal and is sent back home to England while the politicians carve up the Middle East, sowing the seeds of sectarian strife that are still with us today. After cheating death countless times in the desert, Lawrence perishes in a random motorcycle accident on a British motorway.

Martyr characters

Martyrs are distinct from rebels in that they're fighting for a cause that's bigger than themselves and, moreover, they know they're likely going to be killed by the forces that oppose them. Martyrs also tend to have narcissistic tendencies that create conflict with their family and their inner circle. These characters are both noble and flawed.

FILM EXAMPLES OF
MARTYR CHARACTERS

CONTEMPORARY FILMS

Children of Men

In a dystopian future where no new babies have been born for eighteen years, Theo (Clive Owen) learns that his estranged wife Julian (Julianne Moore) is pregnant. Dodging government troops and partisan militias, Theo risks his life to escort Julian to rendezvous with a ship that will transport her to an island where scientists are tackling infertility. As they're about to board the ship, Theo reveals that he's been shot. As his life ebbs away, he instructs Julian how to take care of the baby, bent on giving the world some kind of future.

Milk

In 1977, gay political activist Harvey Milk (Sean Penn) is elected to the San Francisco Board of Supervisors, where he fights for gay rights and against the bigotry in Proposition 6, which would ban gays and lesbians from working in California schools. His devotion to the cause wreaks havoc in his personal life, which is cut short when embittered supervisor Dan White (Josh Brolin) assassinates Milk and Mayor Moscone. As one of the first openly gay elected politicians in the United States, Milk opened doors and minds thanks to his courage.

CLASSIC FILMS

Gandhi

In the early 1900s, Mohandas Gandhi (Ben Kingsley) fights for India's independence from colonial Britain, insisting that his followers employ only nonviolence. Independence is won; however, it leads to India's partition along religious lines, resulting in the creation of Pakistan. Gandhi tries to broker peace between the two nations, angering radicals on both sides, which culminates in his assassination in 1948. While his legacy of nonviolence is still venerated, tensions remain between India and Pakistan.

Malcolm X

Petty criminal Malcolm Little (Denzel Washington) converts to Islam in prison and becomes radicalized as he confronts racial intolerance. Changing his name to Malcolm X, he becomes the face of the Nation of Islam and preaches a doctrine of separation from white society. However, his beliefs soften after a pilgrimage to Mecca and he decides to distance himself from the Nation of Islam. For his perceived betrayal, he's assassinated by Black Muslim fanatics in a New York City church in 1965.

Psychologically damaged characters

These characters have had an intensely negative life experience that has saddled them with profound psychological problems, and it's their struggle to overcome their mental illness and reclaim their lives that's the primary focus of these stories.

Returning combat veterans with PTSD are regrettably a contemporary topic. Other examples are rationalists who have witnessed or experienced inexplicable phenomena; traumatized victims of rape or sexual abuse; guilt-ridden survivors of air crashes; and emotionally devastated survivors of genocide.

FILM EXAMPLES OF
PSYCHOLOGICALLY DAMAGED CHARACTERS

CONTEMPORARY FILMS

Lars and the Real Girl

Lars Lindstrom (Ryan Gosling) has social anxiety stemming from an unhappy childhood. To cope with his loneliness, he orders an inflatable sex doll that he introduces around town as his new girlfriend "Bianca." When the townsfolk realize he's completely serious, they play along, hoping it will help him to heal. When Lars then develops a crush on his coworker Margo (Kelli Garner), it's not long before Bianca "takes ill" and passes away, leaving Lars available to pursue a more conventional romantic relationship with Margo.

Silver Linings Playbook

Pat Solitano (Bradley Cooper) and Tiffany Maxwell (Jennifer Lawrence) are each coping with personal loss and mental illness. Pat, diagnosed as bipolar, is trying to be on his best behavior so he can reconcile with his wife Nikki. Tiffany, a police widow and recovering sex addict, has decided to enter a dance competition. The two make a deal to help each other achieve their goals and in the process, despite their emotional challenges, they fall in love.

We Need to Talk About Kevin

In this difficult film to watch, Eva Khatchadourian (Tilda Swinton) is tormented by the fact that her son Kevin (Ezra Miller) is a school shooter, having used a bow and arrows to kill classmates. Battling depression, Eva's almost grateful for the scorn and abuse she receives from the angry townsfolk. She scans her memories for answers as to how she could have raised such a monster. As her son's eighteenth birthday approaches and he faces a transfer from juvenile to adult prison, she senses his fear. She decides that her only option is to be a mother and so she shows him love in the hope that he might respond in kind.

CLASSIC FILM

Ordinary People

Young Conrad Jarrett (Timothy Hutton) is filled with guilt and anxiety. He's abandoned his friends and his relationship with his parents is strained after a suicide attempt. He begins to consult a psychiatrist, Dr. Berger (Judd Hirsch), and they work to understand that Conrad has been traumatized by a boating accident where his older brother drowned. Conrad learns to forgive himself for what happened, but regrettably his mother cannot do the same. His parents end up separating, which Conrad accepts without blaming himself.

Characters with blind ambition

These characters—typically young adults—have a chip on their shoulder. They've got something to prove and will stop at nothing until they succeed. Working against them may be their age, gender, race, sexual orientation, economic/social circumstances or their own hubris. Often they achieve what they want only to find that it isn't what they thought it would be, and they end up either disillusioned and/or chastened, yet hopefully wiser. Or in films with darker visions, they succeed despite all their moral and ethical failings.

FILM EXAMPLES OF
CHARACTERS WITH BLIND AMBITION

CONTEMPORARY FILMS

The Devil Wears Prada
Aspiring journalist Andrea Sachs (Anne Hathaway) lands a job as an assistant to Miranda Priestly (Meryl Streep), the tyrannical editor of *Runway* magazine, who expects her employees to be at her beck and call. Besotted by the glamor, Andrea embraces the fashion world, which causes friction with her boyfriend Nate (Adrian Grenier), who doesn't like the person she's becoming. On a trip to Paris, Miranda declares that she and Andrea are cut from the same cloth, prepared to make the sacrifices necessary to rise to the top, whatever the cost. Aghast, Andrea quits her job, reconciles with Nate and finds work at a small newspaper.

The Founder
In the 1950s, traveling salesman Ray Kroc (Michael Keaton) buys into the McDonald brothers' prototype concept of a fast food restaurant, agreeing to give them approval over all details of the new franchises. As the restaurant chain grows and Ray struggles with thin profit margins, he tries to renegotiate his deal, but the brothers won't compromise. Ray begins to buy land and lease it

to franchise owners, which is more lucrative. When the brothers challenge him, he works out a deal to buy them out, but then stiffs them on their royalties. McDonalds becomes the largest restaurant company in the world.

Nightcrawler

Louis Bloom (Jake Gyllenhaal) is a lowlife thief who happens upon the aftermath of a car crash and notices freelance cameramen gathering news footage. He decides on a career change and strikes a deal with a TV news director (Rene Russo) to provide her with footage of car crashes in return for money and sex. His business grows and he hires an assistant. When he starts to tamper with crime scenes in order to sensationalize his footage, his assistant threatens to expose him. After they film a police chase that ends in a crash, the assistant is shot and killed by one of the fugitives, who in turn is killed by the police. Bloom has filmed everything, having allowed his assistant to be killed (and thereby silenced) while ensuring that he won't be found culpable. The police are suspicious, but can't prove anything. Bloom hires more assistants and expands his business. For this nightcrawler, crime pays.

The Social Network

Harvard undergraduate Mark Zuckerberg (Jesse Eisenberg) invents Facebook in partnership with his best friend, Eduardo Saverin (Andrew Garfield). As the website's popularity explodes, attracting venture capital investors, Zuckerberg becomes convinced that Saverin is holding the enterprise back, so he reduces his friend's shareholdings, triggering a lawsuit. A legal settlement is reached that leaves Zuckerberg in control of Facebook, but his friendship with Saverin is over and he must live with the consequences.

Whiplash

Andrew Neiman (Miles Teller) has visions of greatness as a jazz drummer. He's studying at the prestigious Shaffer Conservatory under Terence Fletcher (J. K. Simmons), a sadistic teacher who's bent on humiliating and breaking students as a way of separating the wheat from the chaff. Andrew gets revenge on Fletcher by ratting him out, resulting in Fletcher's dismissal. Pretending he doesn't know who turned him in, Fletcher asks Andrew to play at a concert, where he switches the song list to make Andew look bad. Andrew turns the tables on Fletcher by getting the band to play the difficult song "Caravan," and he blows away everyone with his performance, including Fletcher, who's gratified to have discovered a student with the promise of greatness. His father, Jim, however, has deep reservations about his son's choices.

CLASSIC FILMS

The Fly

Seth Brundle (Jeff Goldblum) is a brilliant and eccentric genius. He's in the process of perfecting a teleportation machine. When he eventually solves how to teleport humans, it will be the discovery of the ages. He meets and falls in love with reporter Veronica Quaife (Geena Davis). Despite her concerns, after successfully teleporting primates, he decides to test the machine on himself. He doesn't notice that a fly has entered the chamber and the two are fused during the teleportation process. As a result, Seth slowly transforms into "Brundlefly," essentially becoming a hideous monster. In the end, accessing his last ounce of humanity, he begs Veronica to kill him, and in an act of mercy, she complies.

Wall Street

Ambitious and aggressive young stockbroker Bud Fox (Charlie Sheen) idolizes high-rolling corporate raider Gordon Gekko (Michael Douglas), whose unabashed credo is "Greed is good." Raised in an honest, hard-working blue-collar family, Bud is eager to show his father Carl (Martin Sheen), an airline mechanic, that he will out-earn him. Carl decries his son's ethics as Fox conspires with Gekko to provide insider information; however, when Gekko's schemes threaten Carl's livelihood, Fox must decide where his loyalties truly lie.

Notorious characters

These characters are shameless rascals. They push the envelope of the law, ethics, and morality, usually to enrich themselves in some way, leaving plenty of scorched earth behind them. Having massive egos, they usually also enjoy public notoriety.

At some point, everything craters and they're left with less than what they started out with, sadder but hopefully wiser.

Some learn and mend their ways, while others don't and are doomed to repeat their mistakes or, in certain cases, are *actually* doomed.

NOTORIOUS CHARACTERS

CONTEMPORARY FILMS

American Made

TWA pilot Barry Seal (Tom Cruise) is recruited by the CIA to take surveillance photos in Central America. Soon he begins to transport drugs for the Medellin Cartel to a small town in Kansas, from which the drugs are distributed throughout the United States. He starts playing both sides of the fence by also moving arms to the Contras for the CIA. But soon some government agencies turn on Barry and he also becomes a liability to drug czar Pablo Escobar. One night, Barry is murdered in a motel parking lot.

The Wolf of Wall Street

Based on a true story that encapsulates everything that's wrong with Wall Street, Jordan Belfort (Leonardo DiCaprio) masters the technique of hard selling penny stocks and makes a small fortune. He bends the rules to further enrich himself and hosts a nonstop party that lasts several years. Given a chance to get out of the game before he's caught, instead he doubles down. Eventually, his partner betrays him, and Belfort ends up in jail. Following his release, he's prohibited from selling stocks and relegated to giving hotel sales seminars.

CLASSIC FILMS

A Clockwork Orange

In a dystopian future where ultra-violence is endemic, Alex Delarge (Malcolm McDowell) and his gang of droogs wreak havoc during a sadistic crime spree, which culminates in the murder of a wealthy woman. Alex is incarcerated and brainwashed with "aversion therapy." Deemed rehabilitated, he's released and gets a taste of his own medicine when his victims exact revenge. Unable to defend himself, he ends up in the hospital. As compensation, the government offers Alex a P.R. job, unaware that his therapy has been erased and that he's already fantasizing about returning to his former lifestyle of violence and mayhem.

Bugsy

Benjamin "Bugsy" Siegel (Warren Beatty) is a ruthless mobster. He's also a visionary who sees the potential of a gambling mecca in Las Vegas, and he talks his mob partners in New York into backing the venture. Siegel commences the construction of the Flamingo hotel, but his insistence on extravagant decor balloons the budget to $6 million. When opening night flops and it's also discovered that $2 million of the money has been embezzled by Siegel's girlfriend, Virginia Hill (Annette Bening), Siegel's backers order him murdered. Ironically, over time, their $6 million investment will generate revenues in excess of $100 billion.

Obsessive characters

Intense and driven, these characters are laser-focused on a specific objective, and they won't give up until they achieve it. Anyone who stands in their way risks being mowed down, because for these characters, the end always justifies the means.

Often they're tragic figures, as they forsake so much of their personal lives in the name of the pursued object that when all is said and done, they're left with nothing but emptiness. In some cases, their obsession is so all-consuming that they themselves are destroyed.

FILM EXAMPLES OF
OBSESSIVE CHARACTERS

CONTEMPORARY FILMS

The Walk

What does an artist want? To paint on the world's largest canvas, of course, and French street performer Philippe Petit (Joseph Gordon-Levitt) is an artist. The moment he learns about the construction of the World Trade Center towers in Manhattan, he becomes obsessed with crossing between them on a wire tightrope. The meticulous planning for the stunt takes years and after overcoming countless challenges, Petit achieves his dream, but then is arrested. A judge drops all charges after Petit agrees to perform for kids in Central Park.

Zero Dark Thirty

CIA analyst Maya (Jessica Chastain) is single-minded in her pursuit of Osama bin Laden. She has nothing else in her life, and so at the end of the story, as she walks away after viewing bin Laden's bullet-ridden body, we can't help but think that she seems lost, as if her obsession was the only thing she had that gave her life any meaning. There doesn't even seem to be any glory or satisfaction for her in the "win." If there were a thought-balloon above her head at this moment, it might say, "*Now* what?"

CLASSIC FILM

Moby Dick

Based on the classic novel by Herman Melville, the film tells the story of Captain Ahab (Gregory Peck), who was almost killed by a great white whale, which he named Moby Dick. Out for revenge, his obsession to kill the whale is so great that it eventually results in his own death, as well as the deaths of all but one member of his ill-fated crew.

Underdog characters

Who doesn't root for the underdog? There's something satisfying in witnessing David slay Goliath. This can take many forms: the poor prevail over the rich, the weak over the strong, the minority over the majority. Perhaps these stories are popular because in real life, rarely does the underclass prevail over rich and powerful interests.

FILM EXAMPLES OF
UNDERDOG CHARACTERS

CONTEMPORARY FILMS

Erin Brockovich

Erin Brockovich (Julia Roberts) is an unemployed single mother with three children. She convinces lawyer Ed Masry (Albert Finney) to hire her as an investigator. He gives her a file involving clients who believe their health has been damaged by a Pacific Gas & Electric (PG&E) plant. Brockovich uncovers evidence of hundreds of working people living in the area having serious health problems due to leaking hexavalent chromium from the plant. She and Masry file a class-action lawsuit on their behalf, and when Brockovich finds evidence of a cover-up at the highest levels of PG&E, the company is ordered by the court to pay a $333 million settlement to the victims, who are eternally grateful to Brockovich.

Hairspray

Tracy Turnblad (Nikki Blonsky) isn't part of the "in" crowd in Baltimore in the late 1950s/early 1960s due to her full figure. Undaunted, she auditions to become one of the dancers on the Corny Collins TV show. Collins (James Marsden) hires her, and she becomes an icon for marginalized teens. When she finds out the TV station is going to cancel "Negro Day," she participates in a protest, which results in the racial integration of the TV show.

I, Tonya

Tonya Harding (Margot Robbie) aspires to be a world-class figure skater; however, she comes from hardscrabble beginnings and her reality includes a cruel mother (Allison Janney), abusive husband (Sebastian Stan), and overt hostility from the figure skating establishment. Apparently without her knowledge, her husband conspires to hobble her primary competitor, Nancy Kerrigan (Caitlin Carver). Banned from figure skating, Tonya takes up boxing, only to be further vilified by sports fans. Despite all her personal challenges and bad choices, Tonya became the first American female figure skater to land a triple axel jump in competition and at one point in time was the best female figure skater in the world.

Slumdog Millionaire

In India's infamous caste system, one can't get much lower than a slumdog. So the idea that Jamal Malik (Dev Patel) might win a million dollars on a popular TV game show is something we can get behind, especially as we witness flashbacks of his life that show us what he's had to overcome as well as how he knows the answers to the questions posed in the game show. His life experiences, though difficult, are the key to his success. And he gets the girl, too.

CLASSIC FILMS

The Natural

In the 1930s, Roy Hobbs (Robert Redford), a baseball player in his mid-30s, shows up at the major league New York Knights with a $500 contract from the owner. At first he's the butt of a lot of age-related jokes, but his hitting and pitching soon quiet his critics. Clearly he was a phenomenal prospect at one time, but something happened that kept him away from the game until now. The mystery is eventually revealed and although he's threatened, Hobbs refuses to throw the big game, instead hitting a home run to win the championship.

Rudy

Based on a true story, Rudy Ruettiger (Sean Astin) is a walk-on for Notre Dame's football team. Short at 5'6", he spends his whole time in school on the practice squad until his final game, where he gets in for three plays and sacks the quarterback. After the final whistle, recognizing his determination, his teammates carry him off the field on their shoulders.

Odds-defying characters

These characters are all about tenacity and improvisation. Everything is stacked against their success or survival. Somehow by summoning resources even they don't know they have, they pull it off, usually by the skin of their teeth. We love this "never say die" attitude, and we are there right beside them as they figure out every move.

FILM EXAMPLES OF
ODDS-DEFYING CHARACTERS

CONTEMPORARY FILMS

Cast Away
Chuck Noland (Tom Hanks) is a victim of a plane crash that leaves him stranded on an isolated island in the Pacific Ocean with limited resources. He learns to survive and spends four years there, befriending a volleyball to keep his sanity, until he's finally able to make an escape attempt. He's rescued by a cargo ship and returns home to find that his former fiancée has since married and his old life is now a memory. In the end, he literally finds himself at a crossroads, deciding which direction he should take.

Lincoln
In the waning months of the Civil War, Abraham Lincoln (Daniel Day-Lewis) wants to get the Thirteenth Amendment passed, which will ban slavery. Despite advice that he should wait until he's assured of all the votes needed to pass the amendment, Lincoln is adamant that the issue of slavery be settled before the war is concluded. In the face of fierce opposition, Lincoln is able to appeal to people's "better angels" and the vote narrowly passes.

The Martian
Astronaut Mark Watney (Matt Damon) is stranded on Mars after he's mistakenly left for dead by his crew, who fled the planet during a powerful storm. Injured, with limited supplies and no way to

contact NASA, Mark faces grim odds. A botanist by training, he begins to "work the problem." Blessed with skills and ingenuity, Watney defies the odds and manages to survive long enough to be rescued by his crewmates after eighteen months alone on Mars.

CONTEMPORARY AND CLASSIC FILMS

Gravity, Apollo 13

Both stories are about a catastrophic event in outer space and how, against all odds, the protagonists manage to survive. In *Gravity*, biomedical engineer Dr. Ryan Stone (Sandra Bullock) is on her first mission when rogue satellite debris wipes out the space station and space shuttle. In *Apollo 13*, after an oxygen tank explodes, astronaut Jim Lovell (Tom Hanks) and his crew have to slingshot their spacecraft around the moon to make it back to Earth, which has never been done before. In both films, the characters' ability to improvise and to never give up enables them to return safely to Earth.

Innovative characters

These characters are visionaries. They see things that don't yet exist and bring them into being. Or they do something old in an entirely new way, defying convention and inviting controversy. We admire their moxie and their confidence. Paradoxically, while what they achieve is miraculous, as human beings they are often as flawed as anyone. This gives us hope that we too could be innovators and perhaps are just one good idea away.

FILM EXAMPLES OF
INNOVATIVE CHARACTERS

CONTEMPORARY FILMS

The Imitation Game

During World War II, mathematics professor Alan Turing (Benedict

Cumberbatch) is recruited to the effort to solve the German cipher code that's utilized by Enigma machines. Socially awkward and compensating with arrogance, Turing makes few friends among the team at Bletchley Park. He fights to get funding for an early type of computer, which he programs to crack Enigma. Persecuted for being a homosexual, he concludes that perhaps it's fitting that so-called abnormal people can imagine and see things in ways that others cannot.

Moneyball

Challenged by his limited budget, Oakland A's baseball manager Billy Beane (Brad Pitt) hires an economist (Jonah Hill) and together they determine that statistically, their team has a better chance of winning if the hitters just get on base, even via walks. His theory is deemed heresy by the baseball establishment, but he proves them wrong when the team turns its season around, winning more consecutive games than any other major league team has ever won before, and in so doing, the team unexpectedly reaches the playoffs.

CLASSIC FILMS

Tucker: The Man and His Dream

In the 1950s, Preston Tucker (Jeff Bridges) builds an innovative car that's safer than any other vehicle on the market. Because of this, he becomes a threat to the "Big Three" US automakers and they force him out of business. The film has a great moment when Tucker argues in a courtroom that if we don't let the little guys innovate, then one day we'll be buying our cars from the Japanese, which elicits smug guffaws from the gallery.

Seriously deluded characters

Unless these characters appear in a comic film, they're mostly tragic figures, as what they think will bring them happiness will only bring them misery, and by the time they realize this, it's too late. The audience often has a greater awareness of the situation, and so when the character falters, the audience is validated. They think, "Told you so."

FILM EXAMPLES OF

SERIOUSLY DELUDED CHARACTERS

CONTEMPORARY FILMS

Florence Foster Jenkins

Florence Foster Jenkins (Meryl Streep), a 1940s New York socialite, donates generously to musical causes; however, we also learn that she's secretly suffering from incurable syphilis. This has caused her to believe that she can sing when she is, in fact, a terrible singer. Her husband, St. Clair Bayfield (Hugh Grant), benevolently tries to preserve her delusion by bribing reviewers and papering audiences with free tickets. Eventually, she reads a scathing review that sends her into a tailspin. Bedridden, she acknowledges her absence of talent, yet concludes that while she may not be much of a singer, at least she *did* sing and in so doing, lived her dream.

The Informant

Affable Mark Whitacre (Matt Damon) is an inveterate liar who becomes an informant for the FBI. The Bureau is trying to catch his corporate employer Archer Daniels Midland in a price fixing scheme. Whitacre is caught up in the fantasy that he will take over the company after its current management is fired, but it soon comes to light that he's been embezzling funds. Sent to jail, he's visited by one of his FBI handlers, who feels sorry for him until he realizes that Whitacre is still self-deluded and lying about his misdeeds. He's incorrigible.

Thank You for Smoking

Nick Naylor (Aaron Eckhart) is a smooth-talking lobbyist for a tobacco industry lobby firm who's tutoring his son about freedom of speech. He's convinced himself that his actions in promoting smoking are what makes America great. However, when he's seduced by a reporter and she prints an exposé of his activities, he's fired. He falls into a depression until his son reminds him that he does important work by defending people whom no one else will defend. Reinvigorated, Naylor starts his own lobbying firm. He's glad to no longer be defending Big Tobacco, but he's now looking forward to representing mobile-phone makers against claims that their products cause brain cancer. Some things never change.

Up in the Air

Ryan Bingham (George Clooney) is a corporate executive who travels around the country laying off employees at companies that are downsizing. While he professes empathy, he has none. In his personal life, he practices a philosophy of no "excess baggage." On his travels, he meets a female executive named Alex (Vera Farmiga) and, ignoring his own philosophy, he falls in love. However, when he pays her a surprise visit, he discovers that she's married with a family and for her, he's only been an out-of-town diversion, which breaks his heart.

CLASSIC FILMS

A Streetcar Named Desire

Blanche DuBois (Vivien Leigh) arrives in New Orleans to live with her sister Stella (Kim Hunter), but isn't welcomed by Stella's blue-collar husband Stanley Kowalski (Marlon Brando). A faded beauty, Blanche has been fired from her teaching job for immoral behavior and her lies and delusions are what sustain her fragile sanity. Stanley decries her hypocrisy, yet is oblivious to his own, as while he deems himself authentic, he's really just a brute. In the end, unable to cope with reality, Blanche loses her sanity and is shipped off to a mental institution, leaving to Stanley reclaim his territory.

Fight Club

The narrator (Edward Norton) is an insomniac who's been deadened by his morally ambiguous job and meaningless existence. His drab life is disrupted when he meets an anarchist named Tyler Durden (Brad Pitt). They establish a fight club, where men beat each other up to achieve catharsis from their anger over feminization by consumer culture. This aggression morphs into acts of random destruction of property as they enrol participants and rename their undertaking Project Mayhem. Ultimately, the narrator realizes with shock that Durden isn't real but in fact is a product of the narrator's own psychosis. Having unleashed this monster, the narrator tries to kill himself and thereby kill Durden, but he survives the suicide attempt and the anarchy that he's unleashed continues unabated.

Characters who need redemption

These characters have done something terrible in their past (or the present), and they know it. Initially, they try to live with their deed, but they soon realize they can't and must somehow make amends. So either they take it upon themselves to right the wrong, or if it is too late to do so, then at least they finally take responsibility for their actions.

We relate to these movies because we've all done things we regret. When we think upon them, we wince and wish there were a way we could make amends. Sometimes there is, and sometimes there isn't, so we really appreciate when worthy characters get second chances, because we wish we had them, too.

FILM EXAMPLES OF
CHARACTERS WHO NEED REDEMPTION

CONTEMPORARY FILMS

Flight

Crack airline pilot Whip Whitaker (Denzel Washington) is an alcoholic who's estranged from his ex-wife and teenage son. On a flight, his passenger jet malfunctions and it's through his extraordinary flying skill that only six people on board perish when they crash land. However he soon comes under suspicion and although his union and its lawyer are able to protect him, for Whitaker, all the lies are piling up. At a National Transportation and Safety Board hearing, he's asked to incriminate one of the dead flight attendants for his own misdeeds. He can't bring himself to tarnish her memory and instead admits he's an alcoholic, ready to accept the consequences. Sent to prison, he's finally sober and grateful for his recovery. His repentance pays dividends when his son visits him, now wanting to know his father.

Roman J. Israel, Esq.

Roman J. Israel (Denzel Washington) is a former 1960s civil rights lawyer who defends lost causes for little remuneration. When his law partner dies and their firm is shuttered, he grudgingly takes a job with a large firm in order to survive. Fed up with being principled and poor, Roman illegally collects a cash reward for revealing the identity of a murderer. When that murderer is killed, Roman flees, fearing for his own life, but before he travels too far, he has second thoughts. He returns to submit an important legal brief that will have huge civil rights implications, but before he can file it, he's shot dead by a vengeful contract killer.

CLASSIC FILMS

Groundhog Day

Phil Connors (Bill Murray) is a Pittsburgh TV weatherman and a self-centered misanthrope. On assignment in the small town of Punxsutawney to cover the annual Groundhog Day festivities, he's trapped by a blizzard and finds himself caught in a time loop, repeating the same day over and over again. Slowly he mends his ways, becoming caring and selfless and attracting the interest of his producer, Rita Hanson (Andy MacDowell). The two of them fall in love, and when Phil shows he's really turned over a new leaf, a new day finally dawns.

Schindler's List

Enriching oneself by war profiteering with the Nazis isn't a great path to sainthood, but in this true story, Oskar Schindler (Liam Neeson) fortunately has an attack of conscience and realizes that he's in a position to save the lives of his workers. He redeems himself by sacrificing all his status and wealth to do the right thing, and as a result, thousands of people who would have been executed instead survive the war. Years later, Schindler and his wife are honored as "Righteous Among the Nations" by the State of Israel.

Characters with faith

Whether or not these characters are infused with religious faith, what they all have in common is an unyielding belief in something despite the absence of tangible evidence. Based on their faith, they're willing to put themselves (and often others) on the line.

Both believers and nonbelievers are drawn to these characters due to their certitude. Aside from a possible belief in a higher power, few of us can say we are utterly certain about anything, so we're attracted to characters who have such conviction.

Unfortunately, our human need to "believe" has also been the source of countless tragedies in which innocents have followed false prophets, often to the death. So stories that feature persons of faith can go either way, depending on the writer's point of view.

FILM EXAMPLES OF

CHARACTERS WITH FAITH

CONTEMPORARY FILM

Hacksaw Ridge

Desmond Doss (Andrew Garfield), adhering to his religious faith, decides he won't kill another human being. Enlisting in the army after Pearl Harbor, he's deemed a coward and cruelly hazed during basic training. But when he shows incredible courage at the Battle of Okinawa, saving seventy-five soldiers, he's not only able to remain true to his beliefs, but also shows that even in times of war, people don't always have to use weapons to be heroes.

CLASSIC FILMS

The Exorcist

Yes, this is a movie about faith, in this case the religious kind. When her daughter is possessed by a demon, Chris MacNeil (Ellen Burstyn) examines every possible rational solution in her search for a treatment. When science can't provide answers, she begins to believe in the supernatural, including the existence of demons. She seeks out an exorcist (Max von Sydow) who, in an act of self-sacrifice, slays the demon and heals the child.

Field of Dreams

Ray Kinsella (Kevin Costner) is a simple Iowa farmer who sees things nobody else can see, such as the entire 1910 Chicago White Sox baseball team in his corn field. A convention of these types of stories is that the protagonists—often nonbelievers—initially think they're losing their mind. Once they open up to the possibility that miracles can happen, their world expands, including, in this case, a reconciliation between Kinsella and the ghost of his father in his younger salad days, before he died a broken man.

Let's stop here. Of course we've only skimmed the surface in terms of the range of **archetypal** protagonists, those who represent universal patterns of human nature. The point isn't to be comprehensive, but rather to provide a sense of how a character can be the inspiration for a story that then evolves around them.

How does this help you if you're stuck? Identifying your protagonist's archetype will give you some important clues to the progression of their **character arc**, meaning the way in which they're going to change and grow over the course of the story.

Situation

Brainstorming writing sessions often begin with the phrase "What if...?" This is doubly so for situation-based stories. A **situation** can be described as circumstances the characters are stuck in and can't readily escape. While situation-based stories can be dramatic, this format is also a perfect for humor, hence the television term "situation comedy."

~~~~~~

FILM EXAMPLES OF

STORIES BASED ON SITUATIONS

CONTEMPORARY FILMS

Florence Foster Jenkins

Manhattan dowager Florence Foster Jenkins (Meryl Streep) and
her husband, St. Clair Bayfield (Hugh Grant), an aristocratic former
actor, have an unusual marriage. She's rich and thinks she can sing
professionally, but she has syphilis, which affects her mind. Because
they can never be intimate, Florence allows St. Clair to have his own
apartment, where he discreetly keeps a mistress. While St. Clair
initially appears to be a gold digger, as the story unfolds, it seems as
if he really cares for Florence, as he goes to great lengths to preserve
her delusion, which he knows brings her happiness.

Situation: Here we have two people in a marriage who have made
   an "arrangement." In exchange for financial support and his
   wife's tacit permission to have discreet liaisons, St. Clair provides
   emotional support to Florence and seems intent on giving her
   whatever happiness she can have in whatever time she has left.
   Predation has evolved into devotion.

The Judge

Hank Palmer (Robert Downey Jr.) is a slick defense attorney in
Chicago. He returns to his small hometown for his mother's funeral.
It becomes abundantly clear that he doesn't get along with his
father, Judge Joseph Palmer (Robert Duvall). Hank can't flee town
soon enough, but his father is arrested for a hit-and-run murder.
Hank must remain and defend him, which dredges up a lot of
old memories and emotions that he would rather leave buried;
however, it's just the tonic he needs to move forward in his own life.

Situation: Hank and his dad despise each other, but Hank feels he
   has to remain in town to defend his father in court. Neither of
   them can disengage until the trial is concluded.

CONTEMPORARY AND CLASSIC FILMS

Captain Phillips, Dog Day Afternoon

In *Captain Phillips*, container ship captain Richard Phillips (Tom

Hanks) is captured by Somali pirates, who hunker down in an enclosed lifeboat, which is towed by a US Navy destroyer during hostage negotiations until Navy Seal sharpshooters finally end the standoff. In *Dog Day Afternoon*, Sonny Wortzik (Al Pacino) and Salvatore "Sal" Naturale (John Cazale) try to rob a bank, but they get trapped inside and take the workers hostage. As they try to negotiate their way out of the situation, thanks to live television coverage, they're turned into urban folk heroes. They make it as far as the airport, where the FBI kills Naturale and arrests Wortzik, who now won't be able to pay for his ex-boyfriend's sexual reassignment surgery, which was his motivation for the crime.

Situation: The taking of hostages is a prototypical "situation"— usually a tense one. The kidnappers and their victims are holed up inside a stronghold, while outside the police surround them in force, unable to risk an assault lest they incur collateral damage.

CLASSIC FILMS

The Odd Couple

Due to financial hardship, two divorced men, Felix Unger (Jack Lemmon) and Oscar Madison (Walter Matthau), are forced to share a New York apartment. One is an allergy-ridden neat freak and the other is a bacchanalian slob, and they drive each other crazy.

Situation: Polar opposites stuck in a situation together for reasons outside their control is a tried-and-true recipe for laughs.

Tootsie, Mrs. Doubtfire

In *Tootsie*, unemployed actor Michael Dorsey (Dustin Hoffman) poses as an actress and gets hired on a TV soap. He soon falls in love with Julie Nichols (Jessica Lange), one of his costars, but he can't reveal to her that he's male, or he'll lose his job. In *Mrs. Doubtfire*, actor Daniel Hillard (Robin Williams) is estranged from his wife, Miranda (Sally Field), so he poses as a Scottish nanny in order to remain close to his children. If his secret is discovered, he risks losing access to his children, because his deception is a violation of the law.

Situation: While both films feature guys in disguise who also happen to have jobs as actors, these situations could involve anyone who's pretending they're someone they're not, then gets trapped, unable to be authentic and honest about who they are.

Arena

An **arena** is a subculture or locale. It's where the story is primarily situated. It can be a place *or* a milieu. This means an arena can be geographical (location), societal (class), social (group), political (system), historical (era) or other milieus.

It may be that an arena is your starting point. Perhaps it's a place with which you have familiarity and you want to tell a story set there. Given this, your characters and narrative will be based on archetypes and events common to the arena.

Same plot, different arena

The identical plot can take place in different arenas. The most common example is Shakespeare's *Romeo and Juliet* and the musical *West Side Story*, both of which tell the story of two lovers who hail from feuding gangs/families—a volatile situation that in both stories leads inexorably to tragedy.

Another example of the same plot taking place in different arenas is the western *High Noon* and the science fiction film *Outland*. In both stories, the sheriff is deserted by his community and left to face down murderous outlaws, who are en route to kill him. He must use his wits to survive without any help from others.

Hell in the Pacific and *Enemy Mine* both tell the story of two combatants who find themselves marooned on an isolated outpost and must cooperate in order to survive. The first film takes place on a tropical island during World War II and involves an American solider and a Japanese soldier; the second film takes place on an uninhabited planet in the distant future and involves an Earth star-fighter pilot and an alien star-fighter pilot.

A more recent example is the science fiction film *Ex Machina*, which is about the secret development of a female android by a reclusive genius. It's a stylish update on the classic *Frankenstein* tale, whereupon the creation turns on its creator. Both stories serve as a biblical metaphor for humankind's relationship with the divine and the punishment we incur for our hubris in thinking we can usurp God's primacy in the creation of life.

The symbols are there

A story may work in one arena but not in another. You'll know your arena is right when the **symbols** you need to enhance your story are all there. A symbol is something that indicates, signifies, or represents an idea, object or relationship. For example, consider Las Vegas movies like *Casino* or *The Cooler*. Imagine these stories taking place instead in a casino on a Native American reservation. The Native American casino has all the same stuff inside, but it just doesn't feel quite the same, does it?

Las Vegas has connotations of sin, tackiness, the mob, infidelity, high stakes, desperation, depravity and the like, all represented by over-the-top symbols like flashing lights, thugs in suits, shrill slot machines, and the dispassionate desert.

What about a youth gang movie? An upscale, pristine suburban neighborhood would lack symbols such as gang graffiti, urban decay, racial tension, police profiling, roaming vermin, open fire hydrants, tar beaches (a flat tenement roof where tenants go to sunbathe), tired-looking streetwalkers, and so forth.

FILMS COMMON TO
PARTICULAR ARENAS

ARENA: GANGSTER

Contemporary films: *American Gangster; City of God; The Departed; Eastern Promises; Gangs of New York; Gangster Squad; Gotti; Live by Night; Public Enemies; Snatch*

Classic films: *Carlito's Way; Casino; Donnie Brasco; The Godfather; Goodfellas; Mean Streets; Miller's Crossing; Once Upon a Time in America; Prizzi's Honor; Scarface*

ARENA: HIGH SCHOOL

Contemporary films: *A Cinderella Story; American High School; Bad Teacher; Bring It On; The Duff; Easy A; The Edge of Seventeen; Elephant; The First Time; High School Musical; Mean Girls; Napoleon Dynamite; Not Another Teen Movie; The Perks of Being a Wallflower; 21 Jump Street*

Classic films: *American Pie; The Breakfast Club; Clueless; Dangerous Minds; Dazed and Confused; Election; Fast Times at Ridgemont High; Ferris Bueller's Day Off; Grease; Heathers; Hoosiers; My Bodyguard; Pretty in Pink; Stand and Deliver; To Sir, with Love*

ARENA: HOLOCAUST

Contemporary films: *Bent; The Boy in the Striped Pajamas; Defiance; The Grey Zone; In Darkness; The Pianist; The Reader; The Round Up*

Classic films: *Escape from Sobibor; Life Is Beautiful; Music Box; Playing for Time; Schindler's List*

ARENA: PRISON

Contemporary films: *A Prophet; Animal Factory; Bronson; Conviction; Escape Plan; The Escapist; Felon; Gridiron Gang; Hunger; Lockout; Starred Up*

Classic films: *Birdman of Alcatraz; Brubaker; Cool Hand Luke; Dead Man Walking; Escape from Alcatraz; The Great Escape; The Green Mile; The Hurricane; In the Name of the Father; The Longest Yard; Midnight Express; Papillion; The Shawshank Redemption*

ARENA: TRAIN

Contemporary films: *The Darjeeling Limited; The 15:17 to Paris; Last Passenger; The Polar Express; Source Code; Transsiberian; Unstoppable*

Classic films: *Murder on the Orient Express; Runaway Train; The Silver Streak; The Taking of Pelham One Two Three*

ARENA: YOUTH GANGS

Contemporary films: *City of God; Gangs of New York; Kidulthood; Paid in Full; Straight Outta Compton*

Classic films: *American History X; Boyz n the Hood; The Lords of Flatbush; The Outsiders; Rumble Fish; The Wanderers; The Warriors*

Common Ground

For clarity, what all of the above films have in common is *where they take place*. Given this, many of the films that are grouped together represent completely different genres. So what exactly is a genre? Glad you asked.

Genre

Genre describes a "type" of story. Examples are westerns, mysteries, thrillers, comedies, romances, and musicals.

Specializing

Some writers have an affinity with certain genres and may happily confine themselves to conceiving stories within those genres. It's not necessarily a bad thing to become known for proficiency in a specific genre, because once you're established, producers will seek you out to work on those types of projects. They may need an original script, an adaptation, or an uncredited "punch up."

Stretching

Conversely, many writers don't want to be pigeon-holed and like to work in a range of genres in order to keep challenging themselves, which is something they would forgo if they worked in only a single genre. Whatever works for you is the right choice.

Starting point

In terms of a kernel, rather than a character or an arena or another type of starting point, in this case you simply want to write a certain *type* of film, probably because you're a fan of that particular genre. We'll take a more in-depth look at genre in chapter 12.

Adaptation

An **adaptation** is a script based on an existing work such as a book, stage play, opera, comic, television program, fable, or myth. The advantage of adaptations is that if the original work has already had commercial success, then there already exists some built-in audience awareness for the material, which for commercial reasons, is deemed a plus.

Respect for the original

The trade-off is that adaptations are often *harder* to write than original works. As the adapter, you want to respect the original work, so you may hesitate to make changes. You also don't want to risk reducing the appeal that made it popular in the first place.

Laziness

Existing material can also invite laziness in the sense that you think a lot of the work has already been done by the original writer. So again, there's a tendency to only "rearrange the deck chairs" by just modifying the source material to make it more screen-friendly.

A chair is not a table

Here's the problem: a chair is not a table and vice versa. Screen-based drama is its own form, with its own specific requirements. With any adaptation, the adapter should use the original work as inspiration, but that's where the obligation ends (and the work begins).

If there are lots of great scenes and dialogue and characters that can be repurposed for the screenplay, by all means retain them. But going in, be prepared to change as many details as necessary to transform the work into a purpose-built screenplay.

An angle

Before you can successfully attack an adaptation, you need an "angle." An **angle** is the overarching concept from which every other creative decision flows. It's how you're going to interpret the source material as you adapt it dramatically and visually.

For example, let's look at the film *A Beautiful Mind,* about mathematician John Nash, written by Akiva Goldsman based on the book by Sylvia Nasar. You may remember the shadowy government agent (Ed Harris) and the British roommate (Paul Bettany).

In the book—which, by the way, is a nonfiction biography—these people do not exist (literally, as of course we learn). In other words, in the screenplay these two characters were completely invented by the screenwriter when he undertook the adaptation. Why?

In adapting the book, it was decided the audience should experience what it's like to experience realistic hallucinations. It's not until John Nash is finally diagnosed with schizophrenia that we, the audience, learn that these characters are imaginary and because we were taken in, we understand how hallucinations can seem completely real.

This was brilliant on many levels. First, it generated empathy for the protagonist. Second, it personified the antagonist of the film, which is Nash's mental illness. Third, by creating a potential threat from the government agent, it ramped up the conflict, which ramped up the drama. Both the book and the screenplay are compelling, yet are nothing alike.

More recently, in the film *Jobs*, screenwriter Aaron Sorkin came up with the structure of having each act of the story revolve around the launch of a new Apple product. This was a novel, yet organic concept that allowed the story to be told in a new way.

FILM EXAMPLES OF
ADAPTATIONS

ADAPTED FROM A STAGE PLAY

Contemporary films: *An Ideal Husband; Chicago; Closer; Dreamgirls; Fences; Frost/Nixon; Hairspray; Hedwig and the Angry Inch; The History Boys; Into the Woods; Jersey Boys; The Lady in the Van; Les Miserables; Mamma Mia!; The Producers; Proof; Rock of Ages; The Woodsman*

Classic films: *Amadeus; Dangerous Liaisons; Deathtrap; Driving Miss Daisy; Strictly Ballroom*

ADAPTED FROM A NOVEL

Contemporary films: *About a Boy; Angels & Demons; The Curious*

*Case of Benjamin Button; The Da Vinci Code; Dear John; The Girl
with the Dragon Tattoo; The Golden Compass; The Help; The
Hunger Games; Million Dollar Baby; The Notebook; Pride and
Prejudice; The Time Traveler's Wife; The Town; Twilight; Up in the Air;
We Need to Talk About Kevin*

Classic films: *A Clockwork Orange; Forrest Gump; The Green Mile;
Harry Potter films; The Lord of the Rings; Sense and Sensibility*

ADAPTED FROM A TV SHOW

Contemporary films: *Baywatch; Charlie's Angels; CHIPS; Get Smart;
The Man from U.N.C.L.E.; Mission Impossible films; Power Rangers;
State of Play; S.W.A.T.; Traffic; 21 Jump Street*

Classic films: *The Addams Family; Dragnet; The Fugitive; Maverick; The
Naked Gun; Star Trek films; The Untouchables*

ADAPTED FROM A COMIC BOOK / GRAPHIC NOVEL

Contemporary films: *Ant Man; Avengers; Captain America;
Constantine; Daredevil; The Dark Knight; Dredd; Elektra; Fantastic
Four; Guardians of the Galaxy; Ghost Rider; Hellboy; The Incredible
Hulk; Iron Man; Kick-Ass; Kingsman: The Secret Service; Man of
Steel; Sin City; Spider-Man; The Watchmen; X-Men*

Classic films: *Batman; Men in Black; Mystery Men; Superman; Teenage
Mutant Ninja Turtles*

ADAPTED FROM A FABLE

Contemporary films: *Frozen; Puss in Boots; Red Riding Hood; Shrek;
Tangled*

Classic films: *Beauty and the Beast; The Little Mermaid; Mulan*

True Stories

Screenplays based on true stories are also adaptations. They
present all the same challenges as writing screenplays based
on existing works, with the added challenge that your characters are based on real people, and in the case of contemporary
stories, they may be alive. Pressure! Regardless, you still have
to find an angle.

〜〜〜

EXAMPLES OF FILMS
BASED ON TRUE STORIES

The Tonya Harding / Nancy Kerrigan scandal: *I, Tonya*

Reporter Kim Baker's experiences in Afghanistan: *Whiskey Tango Foxtrot*

Savvy investors bet against the US mortgage market: *The Big Short*

Boston Globe reporters uncover a child molestation scandal: *Spotlight*

The sinking of the *Titanic*: *Titanic*

The ill-fated *Apollo 13* moon mission: *Apollo 13*

The 1950s game show scandal: *Quiz Show*

The Kennedy assassination: *JFK*

The L-Dopa experiments: Awakenings

Howard Hughes's biography: *The Aviator*

The Oakland A's magical season: *Moneyball*

The origins of Mary Poppins: *Saving Mr. Banks*

Rights

My final piece of advice on adaptations has to do with the business aspect of screenwriting. In my final year as a film student at NYU, we had to make a thesis film and I wanted to do something special. It was understood by all of us that these films would be our "calling cards" as we embarked on our careers in the film industry.

I'd always loved Kurt Vonnegut's writing, and in particular, his short stories. In his collection *Welcome to the Monkey House* is the poignant story "Who Am I This Time?" I adapted it into a short screenplay and made it into a half-hour film.

The good news: I earned my master's degree. The bad news: without securing the underlying **rights**, the film could not be exploited. I discovered this when I received an offer from an educational film distributor, but when I said I hadn't secured the rights to the short story, he sighed and told me to call him back when I had.

I found out that the rights had already been optioned by another producer. An **option** gives a producer exclusive rights to a property for a period of time to see if financing for the film can be raised. I was told that the option would expire in eight months, at which point I could obtain the rights—if no film had been made in the interim.

No such luck. Before the option expired, "Who Am I This Time?" went into production and aired as a PBS special presentation, directed by Jonathan Demme and starring Susan Sarandon and Christopher Walken. I was able to compare my work to their work, and amazingly, it held up. Wow. My distribution deal was DOA, however. ShamWow.

So please heed my advice when it comes to doing an adaptation: obtain the rights to the underlying material in writing, either by acquiring a multiyear option or by making an outright purchase of the rights. Of course, this will entail some upfront cost, but if your screenplay ever gets any serious interest, you'll be glad you spent the money.

PUBLIC DOMAIN

Many older properties are legally considered to be in the **public domain**, which means that nobody owns the underlying rights. This happens when enough time has passed that the copyright lapses, leaving these properties available for anyone to adapt.

The risk of basing your screenplay on something in the public domain is that other screenwriters could be adapting the very same property, and if it happens that their work gets produced first, then your screenplay—no matter how brilliant—will be worthless.

Summary

Let's focus on the positive as we close out this lengthy chapter. We've surveyed a broad sampling of the sources for ideas to provide a sense of where ideas come from, which, as hopefully has become readily apparent, can be from anywhere.

So how can understanding your kernel help you get unstuck? You could check to see if your protagonist represents a certain archetype and if so, whether their actions are consistent with that archetype. Or you could check and see if your story is set in the right arena or if there might be a more appropriate arena. Or examine whether your story is in the right genre. And finally, if you're doing an adaptation, do you have an angle?

We've touched on some elements of craft that we'll analyze in detail later on. But before warping there, let's next examine a fundamental aspect of the screen medium by identifying and analyzing its quintessence: using pictures to tell a story.

2

\\\

The Visual Medium

Movies communicate through images. They are, literally, moving pictures. Showing—rather than telling—is the most effective use of the medium and thus has more impact. It's been said that the purest form of cinema has little or no dialogue.

Some might debate this, but think about it: when characters are talking on film, are you watching their mouths? Or are you watching something else happening onscreen, such as their eyes, or their body language, or things visible in the foreground or background?

One common critique of stuck screenwriters' material is that their screenplays are too "talky." This means that the writer is relying on dialogue rather than images to forward the narrative. One technique to help get unstuck is to scrub through the script and see what dialogue can be trimmed or replaced by onscreen action.

No proscenium
Movies are unlike other dramatic formats, such as stage plays and operas, which are presented on a **proscenium** with an

arched opening that creates an imaginary "fourth wall" separating the audience from the actors and an unspoken agreement between everyone involved to accept the artifice.

The constraints of the proscenium require that a portion of the narrative happens offstage. Think about how many stage plays you've seen where weary soldiers return from a huge battle that they fought offstage. There's no "cast of thousands," for obvious reasons.

Furthermore, stage actors must project their voices to the back row. Film actors can whisper if they want and may employ movements that are subtle and contained, which can be easily captured by a mobile camera and a close-up lens.

Realism

Movies also have a fourth wall, but no "agreement" is required with the audience because they're pulled into the realism of the cinema. And looking to the future, virtual reality (VR) experiences promise to immerse audiences even more into cinematic realism.

A film director can transport us to a distant location, then in the next shot focus on a microscopic detail. The result of these abilities is a level of realism unattainable onstage, where actors have to generally face the audience in order to stand and deliver.

One can obviously become fully absorbed in a live performance, but screen media enable us to disappear into the story in a more immersive way, such that our awareness of our immediate surroundings is minimized.

There might be a time in the future where technology will enable a film to take place inside our heads, like a waking dream. One can debate the merits of that level of realism (which I have, in my screenplay *City General*); however, screenwriters will *still* need to tell stories with pictures, whether or not the images wrap around our entire field of view.

Knowing the power of the camera to capture such detail and scope, stuck screenwriters should review their screenplay to examine how much they employ different staging and angles in support of their story, maximizing the power of the medium.

Naturalism

I'm often asked about the difference between **realism** and **naturalism**. The former is a *representation of reality* and the latter is *actual reality*. Having a motion picture camera photographing nature in a forest with no intervention is naturalism. Filming the story of *The Revenant* in the forest and *pretending* that everything is happening is realism.

A few **avant garde** filmmakers have toyed with naturalism on film, and I will say this about that: interesting things have evolved from such experimentation. But these types of films attract a limited audience since most people who watch movies are looking to experience a story, which means they're probably seeking…realism.

Experimentation

While conventional wisdom has always held that the cinematic fourth wall shouldn't be breached, this now appears to be archaic thinking when considering films such as *Deadpool*, *I Tonya*, and *The Big Short*.

In *Deadpool*, breaking cinematic rules is simply part of the overall irreverence of the film, so all of the asides to camera are tonally consistent. In *The Big Short*, talking into camera is used to deliver exposition in sort of a "f**k you" way, which is also tonally consistent with the aggressive, testosterone-laden personas of the central characters.

And *I, Tonya* promises to tell the unvarnished truth of Tonya Harding's rise and fall as a champion figure skater. Having characters speak into the camera is also tonally consistent with the promise of the film, which might be something like: "Listen up. Ignore what you think you know. I'm going to tell it to you straight."

Photographable

Screenwriters must employ only activity or actions that a camera can photograph. Internal thoughts found in prose do not translate onscreen. Furthermore, description should avoid phrases such as, "he remembered he forgot his keys" or "his face showed anger." Rather, the text should read, "he pats his pockets, then curses" or "he scowls."

Present tense

Note that in both of the above examples, originally the text was in the past tense, but when corrected, it was changed to the present tense. That's because in screenplays, the text is always written in the present tense, as if events are unfolding as we read. She walks, he talks, she pauses, he yawns, she sits, he stands, she smiles...he lists.

Descriptive

Also, be specific. Rather than writing things like, "John is hung over," select an activity or an action that can be photographed. For instance you might write, "John turns on the faucet. It sounds like Niagara Falls. He winces and rubs his temples."

Since this is more descriptive, it's also more interesting for your reader. Bonus!

Imagery

Imagery is defined as "the poetry of images," often involving the use of simile and metaphor. In novels and poetry, imagery is used to evoke a feeling; in screenplays, imagery has multiple functions, with its primary function not poetry, but efficiency.

By that I mean we use fewer details to suggest the whole. When writing text or description in screenplays, be concise. Try to have one word do the work of three words and one sentence do the work of five sentences, and so forth. The director and the actors and the film craftspeople will capably color in the rest of the picture. For example, compare the two descriptions below:

```
INT. TENEMENT APARTMENT — DAY

Two policemen kick open the door and enter,
immediately gagging from the smell. There
are boxes of old newspapers and rusty
appliances stacked up to the ceiling.
Shelves on the wall are sagging from the
weight of old toys, chipped dishes, and
cheap souvenirs. Strewn on the floor are
used adult diapers and doggie waste bags.
```

Or:

```
INT. TENEMENT APARTMENT — DAY

Two policemen kick open the door and
enter. They grimace and cover their noses.
The place is a landfill. The occupant is
obviously a hoarder.
```

Multifunction

Ideally, a piece of text or description can also give us other information beyond just the activity being described. Whenever possible, aim for a straightforward description that gives us multiple pieces of information simultaneously. Here's a quick example:

```
Buford opens a bottle of No-Name beer with
his teeth, spits out the bottle cap, and
grins, revealing a missing tooth.
```

Let's see what can be gleaned from this sentence:

Activity: Buford is opening a beer.

Action: Buford may be trying to either intimidate or impress someone.

Character: Buford seems like a redneck because 1) he drinks a cheap brand of beer and 2) he opens it with his teeth.

Attitude: Spitting out the cap means he's a slob, and his grin suggests he doesn't care what people think.

Economic: The missing tooth says he's probably poor and can't afford proper dental care.

Outlook: Having a missing tooth and opening beer bottles with his teeth suggests Buford probably lives hard.

Intelligence: Buford is likely no Einstein.

The point here is that a lot of information can be layered into one descriptive sentence.

The screenwriting mantra

Everything in the line about Buford is *described*, which means it can be photographed. This is visual storytelling, and it applies to everything you put in the text. So consider adopting this mantra: "If it can't be seen, it won't be onscreen."

3

\\

Three-Act Dramatic Structure

The three-act dramatic structure—in which the story is set up, a conflict arises, and then there's a resolution—has been a mainstay of dramatic storytelling since the time of Aristotle. And for good reason, as we'll see below.

You don't have to employ a three-act structure in a screenplay. What you would be losing, however, is an element of dramatic writing that has stood the test of time. You would also be losing a large portion of the audience who have minimal appetite for what they consider experimental cinema.

Niche cinema

A few films have swum against the tide and enjoyed wide success, and to them I say, huzzah! Good on them. But really it just comes down to odds. Do you want to lower your already daunting chances of success by creating something that's less accessible to general audiences? If so, you'd better be a strong swimmer, as the tide is strong.

Mainstream cinema

For now, let's assume you're an average swimmer. As an opinionated writer, you probably have a healthy resistance to formula, yet you're still probably interested in creating work that gets produced and seen and provides you with some financial remuneration. In other words, you want to learn three-act dramatic structure!

Structure is pivotal

Drama in general and screenwriting in particular are formats in which structure is pivotal. Ideally, each moment leads organically to the next moment, creating a scene that leads organically to the next scene, that creates a sequence that leads organically to the next sequence, that creates an act that leads organically to the next act, and so on.

FIGURE 1 THE STANDARD THREE-ACT NARRATIVE STRUCTURE

Take a look at Figure 1, which captures key elements of the three-act dramatic structure. If you look horizontally along the top of the figure, you'll see the demarcation of the three acts. Lajos Egri, the author of *The Art of Dramatic Writing*, describes the acts as follows:

Act I: Establish

Act II: Complicate

Act III: Resolve

With that in mind, let's examine each act in a bit more detail.

Act I: Establish

Act I is where we set the table. However, a common error is to establish the characters, the arena, the tone, and so on, *without starting the story*. Imagine how boring it is to find out what people do, where they go, and who they know, with nothing else happening. Our job as writers is to reveal these details *at the same time* as the narrative gets underway.

So how do we get the story started? We move quickly to the first complication, a.k.a. the **inciting incident**, which is an event that disrupts the protagonist in some way. A change in plan. Inclement weather. An appointment canceled. Someone dies. Whatever. The point is, the protagonist has to make some sort of adjustment from their routine or plan.

This kicks off a stretch of narrative known as the **rising action**, which is still in Act I. Think of it this way: if everything had gone smoothly for the protagonist (because there was no inciting incident), then they would have continued merrily with their life. Boring.

But now they've been jarred off course slightly, forcing them to adjust, with each subsequent adjustment causing a new adjustment. Now they're starting to wing it. To improvise. They must react to new and unexpected developments. This is the rising action. And what's the result each time they have to make an adjustment? *Conflict.*

Referring back to Figure 1, you'll note the word "conflict" in big letters on the bottom, spanning all three acts. No doubt you know why, because you've heard it umpteen times: *Drama is conflict.* There's no story without **conflict**. Nothing should come easily. Few people should get along. Everything should be a struggle or at least an effort.

Also in Figure 1, if you look along the jagged line, you'll find a word that appears in each act: "obstacles." This is how you create conflict—by erecting **obstacles** that stand between the protagonist and what they're trying to achieve.

Act I ends and Act II begins with an event that spins the story in another direction. You may be asking yourself what exactly *that* means. The answer is this: you'll know it when you see it. It's an instinctive thing, based on the story you're telling. Quite often it involves some sort of big decision made by the protagonist as they react to circumstances at hand.

Let's analyze a couple films, starting with *Rain Man.* We can easily identify the event that closes out Act I, where the story spins in another direction and launches us into Act II. It's when Charlie Babbitt kidnaps his brother Raymond from Walbrook Institution.

This event has a couple immediate ramifications. First, Charlie and Raymond become fugitives. Second, Charlie assumes responsibility for his brother's welfare. Until now, Charlie Babbitt has not shown himself capable of caring about anyone other than himself. This is about to change, unbeknownst to him. See how the story spins?

In *The Fugitive*, Act II begins after the train wreck when Dr. Richard Kimball, convicted of a crime he didn't commit, goes on the lam to try to prove his innocence. In *The King's Speech*, Act II begins the moment Bertie decides to humble himself and take elocution lessons from eccentric speech therapist Lionel Logue.

In the film *Whiplash*, Andrew Neiman wants to be a great jazz drummer, but first he has to survive his sadistic, perfectionist teacher, Fletcher. After Fletcher throws a chair at Andrew, humiliating him in front of his classmates, Andrew retreats to his apartment. His options: quit/transfer to another school *or* show that Fletcher is wrong about him. Guess what he decides. The next sequence is a series of shots in which Andrew practices to the point of exhaustion, his hands bleeding. The story spins into Act II.

Act II: Complicate

Otherwise known as "the middle," most screenwriters agree this is the hardest act to write, for a couple of reasons. First, it's usually the longest section of the narrative, occupying about fifty to sixty percent of the overall page/screen time. Second, it's where the story can drift or become circular in the absence of a clear roadmap.

You'll see in Figure 1 that the protagonist experiences advancements and setbacks on their journey as they continue to confront obstacles. The protagonist takes two steps forward, one step back. Or sometimes they have to zig instead of zag. The point is, not only do few things come easily, but everything gets harder. Things *escalate*.

An obstacle may initially stump our protagonist, but they summon personal resources to overcome it, only to then encounter the next obstacle. Each new confrontation generates conflict, which maintains our interest. We also like seeing the protagonist be proactive and resourceful. We respect them for it and it keeps us involved in their plight.

If there are **subplots** in the story—also known as "B" and "C" story lines—Act II is also where we spend the most time interweaving them with the "A" story line. Subplots can be independent story lines or they can intersect and/or contrast with the "A" story line.

Toward the end of Act II, our protagonist will encounter a huge obstacle—the biggest one yet. In fact, it will be so enormous that it will seem insurmountable. Our protagonist will lapse into a funk, which is why we call this the **crisis,** or black moment. The jagged line on the chart dips downward, since at this point it seems all is lost.

Act III: Resolve

At the beginning of Act III, the protagonist is still stuck and there's a brief lull in the forward movement of the narrative. Then something happens that gives the protagonist renewed hope and the willpower to "pull up their socks" and continue their quest.

This new initiative must be something that the protagonist *initiates*. If it's sourced externally, it will be too random and you'll lose the audience, who will think, "that's way too coincidental!" It's unflatteringly described by the Latin phrase *deus ex machina*, which loosely translates into the "machinations of the gods."

We don't want the gods doing the important work of the protagonist, as that would be too easy and therefore unsatisfying for the audience. The protagonist has to figure it all out for themselves and when they do, we're launched into the balance of Act III.

The new initiative brings us inexorably to the confrontation, or **obligatory scene**. This is where the protagonist faces off with the **antagonist**, which is usually a character, but can take other forms, such as personal demons or Mother Nature.

If this scene is missing, the audience will sense it, like a phantom limb. The protagonist has been dueling and battling with the antagonist throughout the story, so it's incumbent upon us to bring them face to face for the final showdown. This doesn't necessarily mean they duke it out with fists or weapons, but they must confront each other in some way.

The moment when one of them prevails in this confrontation is, of course, the **climax**. The outcome of the story is determined at this point. The quest ends. Most important, the **premise**, the theme of the story or the author's point of view, is proven (more on that later).

The **resolution** or dénouement is the final beat of the story, where the dust settles. The primary and secondary plots are resolved. It also gives us a sense of where things would potentially go in the future if the characters carried on with their lives.

Character arc

One last thing to be explained on Figure 1 is the vertical axis where it says "change." This refers to the protagonist, who as a result of their experiences has undergone personal change, also known as a character arc. It means the protagonist isn't the same person they were at the beginning of the story. They've grown meaningfully in some way.

This is important because the audience has invested two hours of their time in the story, and they would like to feel that it was worth it! If the protagonist undergoes no change, then the audience might feel they've wasted their time. Nothing's been learned.

One exception to this rule is the TV **sitcom** format, in which it's critical to maintain the situation, which means the characters can undergo an experience, but things must return to the status quo by the end of the episode so the high jinks can resume next week.

It's important to note that character growth doesn't have to be seismic. Black doesn't have to turn white and stripes don't have to turn solid. Change can be incremental. Straining the metaphor, white can turn off-white and candy stripes can fade.

Let's revisit *Rain Man*. By the end of the story, Charlie doesn't turn into Florence Nightingale. He's still embittered, just less so. He's also less selfish, which is evidenced by his decision to return Raymond to Walbrook, where his brother will be safe.

The Parking Lot Test

That's three-act structure in a nutshell. In the best writing, the audience will be unaware of these bones and all the craft we employ at the service of the story. Conversely, if the craft is absent, the audience will sense something's wrong, even if they can't identify what.

Since nothing should divert the audience's attention, we can't ever let this happen. Everything in the story must pass the "**Parking Lot Test**." This retro phrase describes the walk back to the car after the movie, when people discuss the film they just saw.

If one of them says, "Wait a minute..." and goes on to describe a logic problem or some other craft issue, and his or her friends nod in agreement, the story has failed the Parking Lot Test, meaning peer reviews and word of mouth for the film won't be so positive.

On the other hand, if a film passes the Parking Lot Test, those who saw it will tell others to go see the film. It's a kick to be the one who "discovers" a good movie. Remember, there's a hunger out there for well-told stories with a clear point of view, so when a film has these qualities, it generates enthusiastic word of mouth.

4

Protagonist

One of the first things to examine when you find yourself
stuck is your characters, especially your central characters,
and in particular your protagonist. If your protagonist is fuzzy,
you may have difficulty knowing what actions they'll take
when confronted with choices and decisions. So let's do some
analysis.

How are characters created?

Some writers like to create detailed character biographies
before beginning to write an outline or a draft, and you may
be one of them. This is fine, as long as you remain open to
change, because characters tend to evolve from draft to draft.

In fact, often they begin as **one-dimensional** mannequins
who are manipulated by you to service the plot. However, as
the script is rewritten and they're confronted by obstacles, the
characters begin to make decisions, and not only do they start
to *drive* the plot, they also begin to show us who they are, making them more three-dimensional.

Three-dimensionality

A **three-dimensional** character is both 1) distinct and 2) complex. While we've seen that there are many character archetypes, no two persons are exactly alike: each is distinct and unique. Even identical twins can be different. A character's complexity becomes evident when you contrast the difference between their character and their persona.

Character and persona

Character is who the person actually is. **Persona** is how the person presents themselves to the world. Complexity arises from the difference between someone's character and their persona.

For example, an insecure man may compensate by being full of macho and bluster. Deep down, he's rife with insecurity, so in order to compensate, macho and bluster have become his persona. If asked to deliver a speech in front of a group of people, he'd loudly put it down, call it a waste of time, describe the group of people as a bunch of idiots, and so on. This is a reflection of his persona. The truth is that he's deathly afraid to engage in public speaking, a fear that's sourced in his insecurity.

Proactivity

Whether the protagonist is male, female, an animal, an insect, an alien, a talking plant, or whatever, they must have an important quality: they're proactive.

This means they're the one in the story that makes things happen, even when they're reacting to events. They drive the narrative forward. Ideally, they're hurtling toward trying to attain their **dramatic objective** and achieve their **personal goal**.

Obstacles are erected by the antagonist and/or their agents in an attempt to thwart this quest. This is the pushback that creates conflict as the protagonist forges ahead. Protagonists are always making decisions—often quick decisions—and *acting* on them.

Even a "reluctant hero"—that is, a protagonist who initially maintains they want nothing to do with any sort of quest—is typically forced by circumstances to get involved and, once they have skin in the game, they're just as proactive as any other protagonist.

Why must a protagonist be proactive? Because it's not very interesting if your central character meanders from scene to scene with no drive or intention. It's difficult for an audience to get invested in someone who's aimless. If the protagonist doesn't care enough to take a bit of initiative, then why should anyone care about them?

One could point out that in life certain types of people are inactive, such as lazybones. But think about it—have you ever noticed that lazy people are incredibly active in their avoidance of work? Paradoxically, lazy people can be very proactive.

In a film like *The Big Lebowski*, Jeff "The Dude" Lebowski is an inveterate slacker who has some really wacko friends; however, in the story, he has a clear dramatic objective: to get recompense for his soiled rug. In the pursuit of that objective, he shows us that his slacker persona belies an innate need to prove he's worthy of respect.

Adding details

If possible, each scene should add something to our knowledge of the protagonist. Having said that, only aspects of the protagonist that are relevant to the story should be revealed during the course of the narrative. Aspects of their character that don't come into play are a waste of time and space. The same rule applies to all the characters.

Undergoing change

As discussed earlier, protagonists must undergo change. A story chronicles the progression of a protagonist's journey from one place to another. In the process, they learn something about the world and/or something about themselves they didn't know before. They usually become more self-aware. More conscious. Evn more authentic.

If your protagonist is going to undergo growth, we should first be shown from where. This means they must be "ready for change" at the beginning of the story. In other words, they're in an unsustainable state, often lacking awareness of their condition. They're on auto-pilot and something is about to knock them off course.

No going back

Once a protagonist has undergone character growth, they can never go back to their starting point. As children, once we learn that Santa Claus is a myth, we never again believe he's real. Or if we're betrayed by someone, we'll never again be so trusting. If dramatized, both of the above scenarios would perhaps be stories about lost innocence.

I should hastily point out that it doesn't always have to be negative lessons that are learned. A character who starts out mistrustful and by the end of the story is able to extend trust has undergone positive change. In these kinds of stories, great things can happen for them (and other characters) as a result of their personal transformation.

FILM EXAMPLES OF

CHARACTER GROWTH

CONTEMPORARY FILMS

The Big Sick

Protagonist: Kumail Nanjiani

Character arc: Kumail Nanjiani, playing himself—a Pakistani-American in Chicago—falls for Emily Gardner (Zoe Kazan). Despite their deep attraction, he fears telling his family that he's dating a non-Pakistani woman and also that he wants to be a stand-up comic instead of a lawyer. When Emily falls sick and is put into an induced coma, Kumail realizes the depth of his feelings for her. His devotion to Emily endears him to her parents, which gives him the courage to stand up to his family regarding his choices. When Emily regains consciousness, she's curt with him for his lack of seriousness, unaware of his devotion. To show he's serious, Kumail goes to New York to pursue his career. One night onstage, he's sees Emily in the crowd cheering him on, proud of him and ready to reconcile.

Character growth: From immature to mature

Dawn of the Planet of the Apes

Protagonist: Caesar

Character arc: After his mother dies, Caesar, a chimpanzee with enhanced intelligence, is raised by Will Rodman (James Franco). When Caesar mistakenly attacks a neighbor, he's placed in a primate shelter, where he's treated cruelly by his handlers. It's here he realizes that apes must fight for themselves if they want to be free. He ousts the alpha ape and masterminds their escape so they can live freely and establish their own society on Earth.

Character growth: From innocent to radicalized

The King's Speech

Protagonist: King George VI (a.k.a. Bertie)

Character arc: Due to a stammer, Bertie doesn't believe he's fit for leadership. By the end of the story, having conquered his disability through sheer perseverance, he gains the confidence to lead.

Character growth: From self-doubt to self-confidence

Up in the Air

Protagonist: Ryan Bingham

Character arc: Bingham is a smug executive who preaches a philosophy of carrying no emotional baggage, which leaves him in control of his life. He doesn't count on falling in love. He's so head over heels that he forgoes his credo, only to be dumped by a woman who turns out to be his exact female counterpart.

Character growth: From smug to humble

V for Vendetta

Protagonist: Evey

Character arc: Because he's so prominent in the story, it seems like V is the protagonist in this film, but does he undergo character growth? Not really. He's an embittered man bent on revenge right up until he perishes. It's Evey who changes from a frightened civilian to a fearless revolutionary.

Character growth: From fearful to courageous

Whiskey Tango Foxtrot

Protagonist: Kim Barker

Character arc: Tired of her humdrum life, American TV journalist Kim Barker (Tina Fey) gets herself transferred to Afghanistan to cover the war. After learning the ropes, she begins to take escalating risks and soon realizes she's putting others in harm's way in her pursuit of adrenaline. Worried this will become her new normal, she ultimately decides to come back home.

Character growth: From nonuser to recovering (adrenaline) addict

CLASSIC FILMS

Awakenings

Protagonist: Dr. Malcolm Sayer

Character arc: Shy workaholic Sayer is testing an experimental drug that awakens mental patients who have been asleep for decades. One of the patients, Leonard Lowe, can't understand why Sayer, gifted with good health, is living like a monk. The drug fails and Lowe returns to a vegetative state, but inspired by his patient, Sayer gets up the nerve to ask his head nurse Eleanor Costello (Julie Kavner) out for coffee.

Character growth: From shy to bold

Chinatown

Protagonist: J. J. Gittes

Character arc: Gittes (Jack Nicholson), a private detective based in Los Angeles, is handed a case where he ends up looking like a fool. He vows to get to the bottom of things, even though he's warned that innocent people might be endangered. Undeterred, he solves the mystery, which results in the death of a woman and the kidnapping of her daughter, something Gittes will never be able to make right.

Character growth: From hubris to regret

Ordinary People

Protagonist: Conrad Jarrett

Character arc: Conrad is a troubled teen, having just moved back home from a mental institution after a suicide attempt. We learn that there was a boating accident where he survived but his older brother, the family jock and favorite son, perished. During psychotherapy, Conrad realizes that he was simply stronger than his brother and he forgives himself for surviving.

Character growth: From guilt to acceptance

Tootsie

Protagonist: Michael Dorsey

Character arc: Dorsey (Dustin Hoffman) is a talented but egotistical actor who's difficult to work with and a male chauvinist. It's only when he poses as a women to land an acting job that he slowly begins to appreciate things from their perspective and, ironically, his television character becomes a feminist icon.

Character growth: From chauvinistic to empathetic

Who are they, exactly?

So we know that the protagonist is someone who is proactive and who undergoes change, but a more fundamental question has yet to posed which is, essentially, *what defines their character*? Humans are complicated and it would be simplistic to reduce their essence to a single word.

However, that's exactly what we're going to do.

\\\\\\\\\\\\\\\\\\\\\\\\\\\\\\\\\\\\\\

Dominant Character Trait

Every protagonist has a **dominant character trait**. It defines who they are and it informs all of their decisions. It may not be the face they show to the world (persona), but it's the true essence of who they are as characters.

The protagonist's dominant character trait should guide their actions in every scene. While a character sometimes acts contrary to their expected reaction to a situation, which is always interesting, their actions can't be arbitrary. There still has to be a logic to their actions that can be sourced back to their dominant character trait.

Here's an example: A mom loves her toddlers and would do anything for them, but they're a lot of work and she's exhausted. One day as she's loading groceries in her SUV at a supermarket, a minivan backs over the leg of one of her toddlers, who's trapped.

The minivan stalls and won't restart. Mom drops her grocery bags and, amped with adrenaline, lifts the rear of the car, a Herculean effort she manifests as she frees her child.

Let's say Mom's dominant character trait is love. She shows that love by caring deeply for her children, perhaps at the expense of her own health. Lifting a car seems completely out of character, given her tired demeanor. But is it? Not if love is her dominant character trait.

If the protagonist attains their personal goal at the end of the story, then this dominant character trait is a virtue. Conversely, if the protagonist fails to attain their personal goal, then this trait is a flaw.

Fatal flaw

In tragedies, we've all heard about a protagonist's "**fatal flaw.**" This is just another way to describe their dominant character trait. In a **tragedy**, their fatal flaw is the quality that prevents them from attaining their personal goal. And so inevitably the outcome is tragic.

Sometimes the difference between a virtue and a flaw is a matter of perspective. For example, most people would agree that healthy curiosity is a virtue. It leads to exploration, discovery, and expansion of knowledge, which are good things.

Others might argue, however, that too much curiosity is a flaw. It may lead people to stick their noses into places they shouldn't, usually with disastrous results for themselves and others. The adage "curiosity killed the cat" obviously exemplifies that point of view.

Contrarians

While a particular character trait can be deemed a virtue or a flaw, some writers' life experiences might have them take contrarian viewpoints. For example, they might argue that honesty is a flaw, not a virtue, contravening what most of us have been taught since we were children. In this world view, honesty can lead to negative consequences.

These stories endeavor to show the real world, where amoral characters actually *do* get away with crime or where the rich get richer and the poor get squashed. These generally darker visions are completely valid if the writer can prove their premise (theme).

Vice or virtue or vice

So to summarize, a dominant character trait can be either a virtue or a vice, but depending on the writer, a vice could be a virtue or a virtue could be a vice. Yikes.

\\

Dramatic Objective and Personal Goal

Every protagonist must have a dramatic objective and a personal goal. These are things they are striving toward and it's what makes them both proactive and want to overcome the obstacles that are arrayed in their path. Some may argue that dramatic objective and personal goal are one and the same; however, I believe they are two distinct things.

Dramatic objective

A dramatic objective is a concrete and usually quantifiable result that the protagonist wants to achieve. Examples would be "winning the championship," or "earning a million dollars" or "stealing the *Mona Lisa*" and so forth.

Personal goal

A personal goal is something that the protagonist needs to prove about themselves, usually through the attainment of the dramatic objective, *but not always*. And because the personal goal is, well, *personal*, for them it's usually quite emotionally charged.

~~~~~~

FILM EXAMPLES OF
DRAMATIC OBJECTIVES AND PERSONAL GOALS

CONTEMPORARY FILMS

Dallas Buyers Club
Protagonist: Ron Woodroof (Matthew McConaughey)
Dramatic objective: To combat the AIDS virus
Personal goal: To prove that my life and all lives have value

Gravity
Protagonist: Ryan Stone (Sandra Bullock)
Dramatic objective: To survive a catastrophic accident in Earth orbit
Personal goal: To prove that I can survive devastating personal loss

The Judge
Protagonist: Hank Palmer (Robert Downey Jr.)
Dramatic objective: To clear my father from murder charges
Personal goal: To prove to my father that I'm worthy of his respect

Lincoln
Protagonist: Abraham Lincoln (Daniel Day-Lewis)
Dramatic objective: To abolish slavery
Personal goal: To prove that people will surrender to their better selves/natures

Moneyball
Protagonist: Billy Beane (Brad Pitt)
Dramatic objective: To assemble a winning baseball team on a limited budget
Personal goal: To prove to my family and myself that I'm not a failure

Phantom Thread
Protagonist: Alma Elson (Vicky Krieps)
Dramatic objective: To remain married to Reynolds Woodcock
Personal goal: To prove that I'm worthy of his love

Room
Protagonist: Joy Newsome (Brie Larson)
Dramatic objective: To protect my son and to survive
Personal goal: To prove that I'm a good mother

Side Effects
Protagonist: Dr. Jonathan Banks (Jude Law)
Dramatic objective: To thwart a cold-blooded murder
Personal goal: To prove that I'm a decent man

Whiplash
Protagonist: Andrew Neimann (Miles Teller)
Dramatic objective: To be an elite jazz drummer
Personal goal: To prove to the world that I'm gifted

CLASSIC FILMS

The Full Monty
Protagonist: Alex "Gaz" Garfield (Robert Carlyle)
Dramatic objective: To earn a living
Personal goal: To prove I'm worthy of my son's respect

Home Alone
Protagonist: Kevin McCallister (Macaulay Culkin)
Dramatic objective: To protect the house from burglars
Personal goal: To prove to my family that I'm not a wimp

Four scenarios

Let's use a fictional example of a protagonist whose dramatic objective is to win a championship car race and whose personal goal is to prove he's worthy of his father's love. Perhaps the father never supported his son's career choice—that is, there's some bad blood. There are four possible scenarios involving dramatic objective and personal goal:

Scenario #1: Against all odds, the protagonist wins the championship race and his father, who always doubted him, rushes up to him in the winner's circle, throws his arms around the protagonist, and whispers, "I love you son." So by winning the championship race, the protagonist has achieved his dramatic objective *and* realized his personal goal.

Scenario #2: The protagonist wins the championship race, but his father doesn't care, leaving the son feeling even more unloved. In this scenario, the protagonist achieved his dramatic objective but failed to realize his personal goal. This is called a "pyrrhic victory" or "hollow victory" and exacts a heavy emotional toll on the protagonist.

Scenario #3: The protagonist loses the championship race and his father approaches him in the pit and cruelly says, "I knew you were a loser," then walks off, leaving the protagonist feeling bad not just about losing the race, but also completely unloved.

Scenario #4: The protagonist is in the lead heading for the checkered flag and could win the race, but he'd have to do something that would put another driver's life in peril. Even though the protagonist believes if he forfeits the race he'll never gain his father's love, he swerves out of the way, preserving the other driver's life, but losing the race.

The protagonist pulls into the pit, dejected, thinking he's lost more than just the race. His father approaches, puts his arms around the protagonist, and whispers, "I love you, son." It turns out his father didn't care about the protagonist winning the championship, he just wanted him to be a good person. So in this case, by making an unselfish choice, the protagonist earns his father's love.

If the writing is good, the audience watching this film will cheer if the protagonist wins the race, or they'll groan with disappointment if he forfeits. But ultimately it's not about him winning or losing the race (dramatic objective).

The moment that will resonate most deeply will be when the father either hugs or rejects the son (personal goal), because if the audience is fully engaged in the story, they'll be empathetic to the protagonist and hopefully be in tears or struggling not to weep.

Antagonist

The antagonist is usually a person; however, antagonism can also be personified in other ways. For example, the antagonist could be the brute force of nature in a survival story like *The Perfect Storm*. Or it could be something internal to the character, such as schizophrenia/hallucinations in an inspirational story like *A Beautiful Mind*.

Dimensional villain

The primary function of the antagonist is to try to thwart the protagonist. Ideally, the antagonist should be more than just a black-hatted villain. It's far more interesting if antagonists have their own agenda; in other words, they have something that they want to achieve that puts them in opposition to the protagonist. Like world domination!

Okay, it doesn't always have to be world domination, but it should be *something*. Not only does this make them more interesting, but it also provides an overarching logic to their actions. Additionally, the protagonist and the antagonist should have opposite attitudes and opinions to amplify the conflict. They both believe *they're* right.

Empathy

To hit a home run in terms of characterizing an antagonist, we'd want to take it to the next level, where even though we want these flawed characters to fail, we *empathize* with them. There's nothing more interesting than an antagonist we actually care about.

One-dimensional psychopaths simply aren't as interesting as three-dimensional villains. We must understand *why* they're wicked and, optimally, empathize with them, while still condemning their actions and rooting for their failure.

We know they mustn't prevail, yet we feel conflicted, because we understand what's driving their actions, and we feel that, given the same circumstances, we might make the same or similar choices, even though we know it would be wrong to do so.

FILM EXAMPLES OF

DRAMATIC OBJECTIVES AND PERSONAL GOALS

CONTEMPORARY FILMS

Catch Me If You Can
Protagonist: Frank Abagnale, Jr. (Leonardo DiCaprio)
Antagonist: FBI Agent Carl Hanratty (Tom Hanks)
Protagonist's dramatic objective: Be wealthy and respected
Antagonist's dramatic objective: Track down and arrest Frank Abagnale, Jr.

Protagonist's personal goal: Prove to his father and others that their family is respectable

Antagonist's personal goal: Show Frank that there are better options than being a criminal

Deadpool

Protagonist: Wade Wilson (Ryan Reynolds)

Antagonist: Ajax (Ed Skrein)

Protagonist's dramatic objective: Get his face fixed

Antagonist's dramatic objective: Kill Wade

Protagonist's personal goal: Prove that he's worthy of Vanessa's love

Antagonist's personal goal: Prove that he's all powerful

The Devil Wears Prada

Protagonist: Andrea Sachs (Anne Hathaway)

Antagonist: Miranda Priestly (Meryl Streep)

Protagonist's dramatic objective: Be a successful journalist

Antagonist's dramatic objective: Be the most powerful fashion editor in the world

Protagonist's personal goal: Prove that she is her own person

Antagonist's personal goal: Show she's strong enough to withstand anything

Gold

Protagonist: Kenny Wells (Matthew McConaughey)

Antagonist: Mark Hancock (Bruce Greenwood)

Protagonist's dramatic objective: Find gold in Indonesia

Antagonist's dramatic objective: Usurp Kenny's gold mine

Protagonist's personal goal: Prove he's every bit the man his father was

Antagonist's personal goal: Prove he's the smartest guy in the room

CLASSIC FILMS

Blade Runner

Protagonist: Rick Deckard (Harrison Ford)

Antagonist: Roy Batty (Rutger Hauer)

Protagonist's dramatic objective: Destroy the illegal replicants

Antagonist's dramatic objective: Extend his lifespan

Protagonist's personal goal: Prove that he's human

Antagonist's personal goal: Prove that all life is precious

Good Will Hunting

Protagonist: Will Hunting (Matt Damon)

Antagonist: Professor Gerald Lambeau (Stellan Skarsgård)

Protagonist's dramatic objective: To have an intimate, loving relationship with Skylar

Antagonist's dramatic objective: To have Will maximize his potential as a math prodigy

Protagonist's personal goal: Prove that he deserves to be loved

Antagonist's personal goal: Prove that it takes genius to know genius

Groundhog Day

Protagonist: Phil Connors (Bill Murray)

Antagonist: God (or some higher power)

Protagonist's dramatic objective: Get the same day to stop repeating

Antagonist's dramatic objective: Keep the same day repeating

Protagonist's personal goal: Prove he's worthy of TV producer Rita Hanson's love

Antagonist's personal goal: Teach Phil a lesson in humility

Tragedies

In tragic stories, the protagonist fails to achieve their personal goal and thus, sadly, the antagonist prevails.

~~~~~~

FILM EXAMPLES IN WHICH

THE ANTAGONIST PREVAILS

CONTEMPORARY FILM

I, Tonya

Protagonist: Tonya Harding (Margot Robbie)

Antagonist: Lavona Golden (Allison Janney)

Protagonist's dramatic objective: Become an Olympic champion figure skater

Antagonist's dramatic objective: Thwart or denigrate her daughter's achievements

Protagonist's personal goal: Prove to her mother Lavona that she's not a loser

Antagonist's personal goal: Prove to Tonya that she can't cut the mustard

CLASSIC FILM

Quiz Show

Protagonist: Richard Goodwin (Rob Morrow)

Antagonist: Television industry (Ron Rich, Martin Scorcese)

Protagonist's dramatic objective: Expose corruption

Antagonist's dramatic objective: Maximize profits

Protagonist's personal goal: Prove that no one is above the law

Antagonist's personal goal: Show that they are beyond the law

Formidable

One final thought about antagonists: they must be formidable. Whether it's their brute strength or the size of their brain or the heft of their wallet, they should be more powerful than the protagonist. They should be stronger, smarter, richer...even more respectable.

The reason is twofold: first, the audience must believe that the protagonist *could* actually be defeated by the antagonist, and second, if the protagonist finally does prevail, it's a far more delicious victory if they've managed to defeat a formidable opponent.

8

0

Obstacles and Conflict

We've established that obstacles are the things that stand between the protagonist and the attainment of their dramatic objective and/or personal goal. An obstacle can be viewed as anything that prevents the protagonist from doing things logically and immediately.

In addition to barriers—that is, things or people that prevent the protagonist from advancing forward—obstacles can also involve less tangible things such as technology not working, mechanical breakdowns, natural hazards, misinformation, and so forth. Obstacles can also be internal, sourced in the psychology or physiology of the protagonist, or obstacles can be external—usually erected by the antagonist.

Internal obstacles are more typical of character-based stories. External obstacles are more typical of action-based stories. All chases involve obstacles, of course. Obstacles can help provide **exposition**, which is information the audience needs

6

to know about people, places, and things so they can follow the story. Every obstacle must be organic and logical.

The actions of two opposing forces—the protagonist versus the antagonist—one erecting obstacles and the other overcoming them—provides conflict, the essence of dramatic storytelling. And as we've already noted, without conflict, there's no drama.

I've actually read a screenplay that had near zero conflict. You can imagine how nice everyone was to each other and how easy it was for the protagonist to get on with their business. As you would expect, despite the writer's best efforts, the story was a yawner.

Exactly how much conflict is appropriate? It may vary depending on genre, but a general answer would be: *as much as possible*. An exercise for a stuck screenwriter would be to assess each scene and see if there's a way to ramp up the conflict if it's lacking.

When there's conflict, the audience is involved in the plight of the protagonist; they watch the protagonist encounter obstacles and push through, around, or over them, only to be confronted with more obstacles—continuing right up until the climax of the story.

FILM EXAMPLES OF
EXTERNAL AND INTERNAL OBSTACLES

CONTEMPORARY FILMS

Dallas Buyers Club
Protagonist: Ron Woodroof (Matthew McConaughey)
External obstacles: The politics of AIDS, ostracism from peers,

an unsympathetic medical establishment, lack of available medication, lack of research on the disease, outdated laws, lack of funds

Internal obstacles: Recklessness, hard living, AIDS, alcoholism, lack of education, self-destructive tendencies, homophobia

Fences

Protagonist: Troy Maxson (Denzel Washington)

External obstacles: Poverty, racism, a brain-damaged son, past parental abuse

Internal obstacles: Drinking, bitterness, adultery, illiteracy, resentment

Gravity

Protagonist: Ryan Stone (Sandra Bullock)

External obstacles: Vacuum of space, weightlessness, loss of communication with Earth, limited oxygen supply, fragments of an exploded Russian satellite that orbit every ninety minutes, fire, freezing cold temperatures, the Russian language, the Chinese language, spent rocket fuel, fiery heat of reentry, heavy spacesuit, possibility of drowning, Earth's gravity

Internal obstacles: Survivor grief over the death of her daughter, panic, grief over the death of astronaut Matt Kowalski, lack of experience in space, a short training period, physical/mental exhaustion

Molly's Game

Protagonist: Molly Bloom (Jessica Chastain)

External obstacles: Her father, the FBI, police, mobsters, cutthroat gamblers, deadbeats

Internal obstacles: Self-doubt, drug habit, being female

Moneyball

Protagonist: Billy Beane (Brad Pitt)

External obstacles: His frugal team owner, an inadequate player budget, selfish players, a culture of losing, the team's "old school" manager, other GMs who negotiate tough player trades, other teams who want to win, his ex-wife's rich husband Alan

Internal obstacles: Self-doubt because he didn't pan out as a player, repressed emotions, difficulty with personal relationships, his temper, superstitions, too much junk food

School of Rock

Protagonist: Dewey Finn (Jack Black)

External obstacles: Unpaid rent, financial debt, his roommate's hostile girlfriend, uptight Principal Mullins, the students' demanding parents, the snooty band competition director, his students' youth and inexperience, a pretentious rival rock band

Internal obstacles: Immaturity, tendency to showboat and sponge off his friends, being an unskilled liar

CLASSIC FILM

Tootsie

Protagonist: Michael Dorsey (Dustin Hoffman)

External obstacles: Dilettante directors, his long-suffering talent agent, lack of money, hostile casting directors, egotistical TV soap director, the father of the actress he loves (who develops a crush on "Dorothy")

Internal obstacles: Perfectionism, being difficult, stubbornness, selfishness, misogyny, deception, unrequited love

Tangible Stakes

We know we become more involved in the plight of a protagonist who's confronting and overcoming obstacles, which generates conflict in the story. However, if there's very little at stake, then the story won't be as compelling. There's two kinds of stakes:

> *Personal stakes* are consequences that will befall the protagonist should they fail to attain their dramatic objective and/or personal goal.

> *External stakes* are consequences that will befall others should the protagonist fail to attain their dramatic objective and/or personal goal.

Both these kinds of stakes need to be tangible, meaning that they have a quantifiable impact. The greater the **tangible stakes**, the more dramatic the story.

TANGIBLE STAKE:

IF THE CONSPIRACY ISN'T UNCOVERED...

CONTEMPORARY FILMS

Get Out

Protagonist: Chris Washington (Daniel Kaluuya)

Personal stakes: I'll have no free will, forfeit my brain, lose my freedom

External stakes: Other Black people will become victims of a racist immortality cult

Snowden

Protagonist: Edward Snowdon (Joseph Gordon-Levitt)

Personal stakes: I'll compromise my principles, lose my citizenship, lose my freedom, lose my life

External stakes: The American government will have unfettered access to monitor US citizens, ending personal privacy

CLASSIC FILMS

A Perfect Murder

Protagonist: Emily Taylor (Gwyneth Paltrow)

Personal stakes: My husband will kill me

External stakes: A murderer will remain at large

The Devil's Advocate

Protagonist: Kevin Lomax (Keanu Reeves)

Personal stakes: I'll become an instrument of the devil

External stakes: The devil will perpetuate evil through his offspring

Enemy of the State

Protagonist: Robert Clayton Dean (Will Smith)

Personal stakes: I'll lose my job, my marriage, my savings, my reputation

External stakes: The NSA will get away with murdering political opponents and a bill will pass in Congress giving the NSA more power

12 Monkeys

Protagonist: James Cole (Bruce Willis)

Personal stakes: I'll be trapped in a dystopian future

External stakes: A lunatic will release deadly microbes in every corner of the planet, ending civilization

---

TANGIBLE STAKE:

IF I DON'T DISCOVER A CURE...

CONTEMPORARY FILM

Dallas Buyers Club

Protagonist: Ron Woodroof (Matthew McConaughey)

Personal stakes: I'll die

External stakes: Everyone infected with HIV will die

CLASSIC FILMS

Awakenings

Protagonist: Dr. Malcolm Sayer (Robin Williams)

Personal stakes: I'll fail my friend

External stakes: My patients will regress back into catatonia

Charly

Protagonist: Charly Gordon (Cliff Robertson)

Personal stakes: I'll regress intellectually

External stakes: Science will won't be advanced

DOA

Protagonist: Professor Dexter Cornell (Dennis Quaid)
Personal stakes: I'll die from a slow-acting poison
External stakes: My killer will get away with murder

Lorenzo's Oil

Protagonist: Michaela Odone (Susan Sarandon)
Personal stakes: My son will die from adrenoleuko-dystrophy
External stakes: Many other kids will die from this disease

Outbreak

Protagonist: Colonel Sam Daniels (Dustin Hoffman)
Personal stakes: My wife will die
External stakes: The next black plague will descend upon Earth

---

TANGIBLE STAKE:

IF I DON'T TAKE RESPONSIBILITY FOR MY ACTIONS...

CONTEMPORARY FILMS

How the Grinch Stole Christmas

Protagonist: The Grinch (Jim Carrey)
Personal stakes: I'll always be reviled and alone
External stakes: Christmas spirit will be destroyed

The Life of David Gale

Protagonist: David Gale (Kevin Spacey)
Personal stakes: I'll never earn my son's love and respect
External stakes: Capital punishment will never be abolished

The Post

Protagonist: Kay Graham (Meryl Streep)

Personal stakes: I will betray my husband's memory and show I'm not capable of leadership

External stakes: Americans will continue to die in Vietnam in a lost cause

Roman J. Israel, Esq.

Protagonist: Roman J. Israel (Denzel Washington)

Personal stakes: I'll betray my principles and become that which I have always despised

External stakes: My groundbreaking civil rights brief will never be filed

CLASSIC FILMS

The Bridge on the River Kwai

Protagonist: Colonel Nicholson (Alec Guinness)

Personal stakes: I'll be a traitor to my country

External stakes: The enemy will gain an advantage and many compatriots will die

Schindler's List

Protagonist: Oskar Schindler (Liam Neeson)

Personal stakes: I'll be a war profiteer and a monster

External stakes: Thousands of Jews will be exterminated by the Nazis

10

\\\

Comedy or Tragedy

Let's take a moment here to make a distinction in terms. When we use the words "tragedy" and "comedy," we're not talking about sad and *funny*. We're talking about sad and *happy*. So for the purposes of analysis, when we use the word "comedy," we're using it in the classical sense, where it means a story with a happy ending. To avoid confusion, throughout this book we'll use the word "comic" to refer to funny films.

Happy and sad endings

I may be risking the Captain Obvious moniker talking about happy and sad endings; however, understanding precisely what it is that you're writing is critical to the process.

Perhaps you've seen a film that was clearly a tragedy, but it tested poorly, so the studio tacked on a happy ending so the audience wouldn't go home bummed out. This rarely if ever works, as the whole point of the film is completely undermined.

Once again, let's look at our race car movie example. There were four possible scenarios involving the protagonist's dramatic objective and personal goal:

1. The protagonist achieves his dramatic objective and realizes his personal goal.
2. The protagonist achieves his dramatic objective, but fails to realize his personal goal (pyrrhic victory).
3. The protagonist fails to achieve both his dramatic objective and personal goal.
4. The protagonist fails to achieve his dramatic objective, but realizes his personal goal.

Based on the classic definition of comedy and tragedy, scenarios 1 and 4 are comedies (i.e., stories with happy endings) and scenarios 2 and 3 are tragedies (i.e., stories with sad endings). Remember, this categorization is determined by whether or not the protagonist realizes their personal goal. If yes—then comedy. If no—then tragedy.

FILM EXAMPLES OF
TRAGEDIES AND COMEDIES

Classic tragedies

A Clockwork Orange	Dr. Strangelove	Quiz Show
Amadeus	Frankenstein	The Remains of the Day
Bugsy	The Godfather	Romeo and Juliet
Charly	Lawrence of Arabia	Tucker: The Man and His Dream
Chinatown	Midnight Cowboy	12 Monkeys
Dog Day Afternoon	Moby Dick	West Side Story

Classic comedies

A Perfect Murder

Alien

All the President's Men

Apollo 13

Awakenings

Being There

The Big Lebowski

Blade Runner

The Bridge on the River Kwai

The China Syndrome

The Crying Game

Dead Man Walking

Dead Poets Society

The Devil's Advocate

DOA

Enemy Mine

The Exorcist

Field of Dreams

Forrest Gump

The Fugitive

The Full Monty

Going in Style

Good Will Hunting

Groundhog Day

Harold and Maude

Hell in the Pacific

High Noon

Inside Man

It's a Wonderful Life

Jerry Maguire

Lorenzo's Oil

Mad Max

Mrs. Doubtfire

The Odd Couple

One Flew Over the Cuckoo's Nest

Ordinary People

Outbreak

Outland

Papillion

Parenthood

Rain Man

Rocky

Schindler's List

The Shawshank Redemption

The Sixth Sense

Terms of Endearment

Tootsie

When Harry Met Sally

Contemporary tragedies

Ex Machina

Fences

The Fifth Estate

Get Out

I, Tonya

The Informant

The Perfect Storm

Roman J. Israel, Esq.

The Social Network

Up in the Air

Whiplash

Zero Dark Thirty

Contemporary comedies

A Beautiful Mind

About a Boy

Avatar

Bad Words

The Big Sick

The Bucket List

Captain Phillips

Cast Away

Catch Me If You Can

Dallas Buyers Club

Dawn of the
Planet of the
Apes

The Devil Wears
Prada

Erin Brockovich

Flight

Freezer Burn:
The Invasion of
Laxdale

Gold

Gravity

Hairspray

Hidden Figures

Home Alone

How the Grinch
Stole Christmas

The Judge

Jurassic Park

The King's Speech

Lars and the Real
Girl

The Last Samurai

The Life of David
Gale

Lincoln

The Martian

Matchstick Men

Moneyball

Nightcrawler

Ordinary People

Passengers

Phantom Thread

School of Rock

Comedies vs. tragedies

You may have noticed my lists of comedies far outweigh the
tragedies. This could be a result of my own bias in terms of
the films I've seen. Or it could be that films that send us home
happy and content instead of sad and unsettled are perhaps
more commercial. The answer probably lies somewhere in
between. But what we can safely say is that many of the films
I've classified as tragedies are among the best films ever made.

Premise

The definition of *premise* we're using was first described by Lajos Egri in *The Art of Dramatic Writing*. He was writing about stage plays, but the elements of three-act dramatic writing also apply to screenplays.

A premise is what the writer is writing about. It is the writer's belief or point of view and it's what they're trying to prove through the telling of the story, without being preachy. The premise can simply be a basic belief. It doesn't have to be a "deep" message. It should just be something that the writer holds to be true.

The premise gives the story a spine. It's a touchstone that a stuck screenwriter can keep consulting, as it provides a way to test every element that's written to see if it's pertinent or relevant. If it isn't, then that element either needs to be modified or discarded.

The premise can be stated in a phrase composed of three words that represent the following: character, conflict, and outcome.

1. The first word describes the dominant character trait of the protagonist.

2. The second word describes the conflict in the story, so it's always an active verb in the present tense.

3. The third word, when amplified by the second word, describes the outcome. To explain, if the dominant character trait of the protagonist is a virtue, then the outcome is usually comedic (happy). If the dominant character trait is a flaw, then the outcome is usually tragic (sad). Either way, the outcome is tied closely to the conflict word.

Let's examine two examples. In *Passengers*, Jim Preston's dominant character trait is selflessness, which is considered a virtue. In the end, he and Aurora find everlasting love, classifying the story as a comedy.

Conversely, in *The Godfather*, Michael Corleone's dominant character trait is ruthlessness. In the end, he attains power and becomes Godfather, but the cost to him is estrangement from his wife, Kay, classifying the story as a tragedy.

In *Passengers*, love is engendered by selflessness. In *The Godfather*, love is destroyed by ruthlessness. Both premises use "love" as the third word, but the third word is *defined* by the second word. In one, love is engendered and in the other, love is destroyed.

Once again we can't forget about our contrarian writers who possess what I've described as darker visions. These writers might pen stories where selflessness destroys love and ruthlessness engenders love. And to boot, they might deem everyone else contrarians!

Frankly, I admire films that challenge me to question my own assumptions. I may not agree with a contrarian's particular point of view; however, if it's a good story well told, I'll always revere their craft. And hey, they could compel me to reexamine my ideas. Good writing can either affirm or challenge our beliefs, and to me, that's a positive thing.

EXAMPLES OF
PREMISES FROM FILMS

CONTEMPORARY FILMS

Doctor Strange
Protagonist: Dr. Strange (Benedict Cumberbatch)
Dramatic objective: Become like a "god" again
Personal goal: Prove that rules are meant to be broken
Personal stakes: His ego, his career, his life
External stakes: Vanquishment of the world by the dark dimension
Dominant character trait: Humility
Antagonist: Kaecilius (Mads Mikkelsen)
Obstacles: Bodily injuries, spells, magic, demons
Comedy or tragedy: Comedy
Premise: Humility trumps hubris

Passengers
Protagonist: Jim Preston (Chris Pratt)
Dramatic objective: To have a companion
Personal goal: To prove to Aurora (Jennifer Lawrence) that he's worthy of her love
Personal stakes: Boredom, loneliness, suicide
External stakes: Spaceship failure, the loss of the other passengers, the colony on Homestead II won't ever be established
Dominant character trait: Selflessness

Antagonist: Time

Obstacles: Isolation, vast distances, vacuum of space, malfunctioning spacecraft

Comedy or tragedy: Comedy

Premise: Selflessness engenders love

CLASSIC FILMS

Alien

Protagonist: Ripley (Sigourney Weaver)

Dramatic objective: To locate and kill the alien

Personal goal: To prove that I deserve respect

Personal stakes: My survival

External stakes: My mission, my crew, the survival of the human race

Dominant character trait: Resourcefulness

Antagonist: The alien

Obstacles: Isolation, vacuum of space, broken machinery, auto-destruct mechanism

Comedy or tragedy: Comedy

Premise: Resourcefulness enables survival

All the President's Men

Protagonist: Bob Woodward (Robert Redford)

Dramatic objective: To get the story

Personal goal: To prove I'm a good reporter

Personal stakes: My job, my life

External stakes: Honest government, the future of my country

Dominant character trait: Skepticism

Antagonist: Richard Nixon

Obstacles: CIA, the White House, Washington power elite

Comedy or tragedy: Comedy

Premise: Skepticism exposes corruption

Amadeus

Protagonist: Antonio Salieri (F. Murray Abraham)

Dramatic objective: To destroy Mozart

Personal goal: To prove that God made a mistake

Personal stakes: The king's favor, my position at court, my reputation, my sanity

External stakes: Mozart's genius will be recognized

Dominant character trait: Jealousy

Antagonist: Wolfgang Mozart (Tom Hulce)

Obstacles: Mozart's brilliance, Salieri's conscience

Comedy or tragedy: Tragedy

Premise: Jealousy causes ruin

Chinatown

Protagonist: J. J. Gittes (Jack Nicholson)

Dramatic objective: To find out who killed Hollis Mulwray

Personal goal: To prove that no one makes a fool out of me

Personal stakes: My reputation, my living, my survival

External stakes: Corruption, malfeasance, incest, murder

Dominant character trait: Hubris

Antagonist: Noah Cross (John Huston)

Obstacles: The police, Cross's henchman, complex conspiracy, Mrs. Mulwray's (Faye Dunaway) secret

Comedy or tragedy: Tragedy

Premise: Hubris creates regret

Dead Man Walking

Protagonist: Sister Helen Prejean (Susan Sarandon)

Dramatic objective: Help Matthew Poncelet (Sean Penn) accept responsibility for his actions and ask for forgiveness

Personal goal: Prove that my beliefs are valid

Personal stakes: The loss of my faith, the loss of my vocation

External stakes: Poncelet's salvation, the victims' parents' peace of mind

Dominant character trait: Forgiveness
Antagonist: Unbelievers
Obstacles: The prison, society's attitudes, date of execution
Comedy or tragedy: Comedy
Premise: Forgiveness promotes healing

Field of Dreams

Protagonist: Ray Kinsella (Kevin Costner)
Dramatic objective: To heed the voice
Personal goal: To prove that I'm not crazy
Personal stakes: My farm, my marriage, my family, my sanity
External stakes: Terrence Mann (James Earl Jones) will remain cynical, Dr. Graham (Burt Lancaster) will never have closure
Dominant character trait: Faith
Antagonist: The bank (Timothy Busfield)
Obstacles: No money, bank foreclosure, the players are invisible to others
Comedy or tragedy: Comedy
Premise: Faith produces miracles

The Fugitive

Protagonist: Dr. Richard Kimble (Harrison Ford)
Dramatic objective: To find my wife's killer
Personal goal: To prove that I loved my wife
Personal stakes: My life (I'm to be executed for her murder)
External stakes: Vascular patients will receive a drug that causes liver damage
Dominant character trait: Truthfulness
Antagonist: Dr. Charles Nichols (Jeroen Krabbé)
Obstacles: US Marshals, no money, on the run, the one-armed man, drug about to be approved by the FDA
Comedy or tragedy: Comedy
Premise: Truth redresses injustice

The Godfather

Protagonist: Michael Corleone (Al Pacino)
Dramatic objective: To protect the family
Personal goal: To prove I'm capable of being Godfather
Personal stakes: My marriage, my family, my power, my survival
External stakes: Crime, assassination, corruption
Dominant character trait: Ruthlessness
Antagonist: Barzini (Richard Conte)
Obstacles: The other godfathers, the FBI, betrayers, changing times, conscience
Comedy or tragedy: Tragedy
Premise: Ruthlessness destroys love

It's a Wonderful Life

Protagonist: George Bailey (James Stewart)
Dramatic objective: To do great things with my life
Personal goal: To prove I have worth
Personal stakes: My livelihood, my marriage, my family, my community, my life
External stakes: Potter will control Bedford Falls, people will become callous and uncaring
Dominant character trait: Unselfishness
Antagonist: Mr. Potter (Lionel Barrymore)
Obstacles: Father's death, Uncle Billy (Thomas Mitchell) losing the bank deposit, bank run
Comedy or tragedy: Comedy
Premise: Selflessness fosters goodwill

The Shawshank Redemption

Protagonist: Andy Dufresne (Tim Robbins)
Dramatic objective: Escape to freedom
Personal goal: Prove that I cannot be "institutionalized"
Personal stakes: My freedom, my sanity
External stakes: Justice, hope
Dominant character trait: Patience

Antagonist: Warden Norton (Bob Gunton)

Obstacles: Prison walls, prison guards, prison rapists, despair, resignation

Comedy or tragedy: Comedy

Premise: Patience yields rewards

"Leads to"

One last thing. It's often challenging to select the conflict word of the premise. So as a stopgap, you can use the phrase "leads to," with the understanding that at some point you'll replace it with a single verb that describes the nature of the conflict in the story.

12

〜〜〜〜〜〜〜〜〜〜〜〜〜〜〜〜〜〜〜〜〜〜〜〜〜

Genre

A train movie

I was introduced to the concept of genre on my first film industry job. I was twenty-one and thanks to family connections and good timing, I got hired as a production assistant on *The Silver Streak*, a comic-thriller starring Gene Wilder and Richard Pryor about a murder on a Los Angeles-to-Chicago train trip.

One day I was talking to one of the producers, Ed Milkis, who had been a producer on the original *Star Trek* series and who would produce some of the most popular TV shows ever made. I asked about the genesis of this project and he replied, "We thought it was a good time to do a train movie."

A good time to do a train movie. I wasn't sure what he meant, but I quietly nodded and later came to understand. He was saying that the time was right to do a certain "type" of story, that is, genre. And a train movie is an example of a genre known as *road pictures*.

In a **road picture**, the protagonist travels from point A to point B, pressured by a deadline. Road pictures can involve any form of transportation, like, for example...*Planes, Trains and Automobiles* (which, of course, is an iconic road picture).

And just to illustrate how you can find a fresh take on just about anything, a few years ago I executive-produced a road picture called *40 Below and Falling*, in which the conveyances used by the lead characters were two snowmobiles.

Subgenres

Many popular genres can be further divided into subgenres.

For the purpose of illustration, below is a sample list of genres and subgenres accompanied by classic and contemporary movie examples. Note: some films appear in more than one category. For example, the film *Snatch* is **black comedy** with a **caper** plot that features gangsters, so it appears in three genre categories.

FILM EXAMPLES OF

GENRES AND SUBGENRES

GENRE: SPECULATIVE

Subgenre: Science fiction

Contemporary films: *The Adjustment Bureau; Annihilation; Blade Runner 2049; Dawn of Planet of the Apes; District 9; Eternal Sunshine of the Spotless Mind; Ex Machina; Gravity; Her; I, Robot; I Am Legend; Inception; Interstellar; Jurassic World; King Kong; The Martian; Moon; Passengers; Repo Men; Sunshine; War for the Planet of the Apes; War of the Worlds*

Classic films: *The Abyss; Altered States; The Andromeda Strain; Blade Runner; Close Encounters of the Third Kind; Dreamscape; Enemy Mine; The Fly; Invasion of the Body Snatchers; Jurassic Park;*

Mad Max; The Matrix; Robo-Cop; Stargate; The Terminal Man; Terminator; They Live; 2001: A Space Odyssey

Subgenre: Science fantasy

Contemporary films: *Avatar; Guardians of the Galaxy; Maze Runner: The Death Cure; Pacific Rim; Ready Player One; Star Trek films; Star Wars films; Transformers*

Classic films: *E.T.; The Fifth Element; Krull; Star Trek films; Star Wars films*

Subgenre: Reincarnation

Contemporary films: *Cloud Atlas; Birth; Origins; Unmistaken Child*

Classic films: *Audrey Rose; Dead Again; Heaven Can Wait; Little Buddha; Made in Heaven; The Reincarnation of Peter Proud; Slaughterhouse-Five*

Subgenre: Time travel

Contemporary films: *About Time; Arrival; The Butterfly Effect; Edge of Tomorrow; Hot Tub Time Machine; Interstellar; Looper; Midnight in Paris; Minority Report; Predestination; Source Code; The Time Traveler's Wife; X-Men: Days of Future Past*

Classic films: *Back to the Future; Bill and Ted's Excellent Adventure; The Philadelphia Experiment; Somewhere in Time; Time Bandits; The Time Machine*

Subgenre: Horror

Contemporary films: *A Cure for Wellness; A Quiet Place; Gerald's Game; Get Out; Godzilla; Hereditary; I, Frankenstein; IT; Life; The Mist; Mom and Dad; Slender Man; Twilight; Underworld; Unsane; Van Helsing; Wilding; Winchester; World War Z*

Classic films: *Alien; The Birds; The Exorcist; Fallen; Jaws; Magic; The Mummy; The Omen; Poltergeist; Psycho; The Serpent and the Rainbow*

Subgenre: Fantasy

Contemporary films: *Alice in Wonderland; The Brothers Grimm; The Chronicles of Narnia; Clash of the Titans; Harry Potter films; Hugo; John Carter; Jumanji: Welcome to the Jungle; The Lord of the Rings; Maleficent; Night at the Museum; Outlander; Pan's Labyrinth; Peter Pan; Snow White and the Huntsman; The Water Horse*

Classic films: *Jason and the Argonauts; The Seventh Voyage of Sinbad; The Wizard of Oz*

Subgenre: Body swapping

Contemporary films: *The Change-Up; Freaky Friday; The Hot Chick; It's a Boy Girl Thing; Self/less; The Swap; Your Name*

Classic films: *All of Me; Big; 18 Again!; Face Off; Prelude to a Kiss*

GENRE: ACTION/ADVENTURE

Subgenre: Quest

Contemporary films: *Blood Diamond; Finding Nemo; The Hunger Games; Ice Age; Lara Croft; National Treasure; The Perfect Storm; Sahara; Up*

Classic films: *The Goonies; Moby Dick; Raiders of the Lost Ark; Romancing the Stone*

Subgenre: War

Contemporary films: *Behind Enemy Lines; Black Hawk Down; Defiance; Dunkirk; Flags of Our Fathers; Good Kill; The Hurt Locker; Inglourious Basterds; Jarhead; Journey's End; Letters from Iwo Jima; Megan Leavey; Pearl Harbor; Sand Castle; 12 Strong; The Yellow Birds*

Classic films: *Battle of the Bulge; Das Boot; Platoon; Saving Private Ryan; The Thin Red Line; Tobruk; Tora, Tora, Tora*

Subgenre: Swashbuckler

Contemporary films: *Blackbeard; The Count of Monte Cristo; The Legend of Zorro; Master and Commander: The Far Side of the World; Musketeer; Pirates of the Caribbean films; Sinbad: Legend of the Seven Seas*

Classic films: *Captain Blood; The Swashbuckler; The Three Musketeers*

Subgenre: Sword and sorcery

Contemporary films: *A Knight's Tale; The Chronicles of Narnia; Gladiator; Immortals; Kingdom of Heaven; Prince of Persia: The Sands of Time; 300; Troy*

Classic films: *Conan the Barbarian; Red Sonja*

Subgenre: Chase

Contemporary films: *Baby Driver; Catch Me If You Can; Drive; Fast and Furious films; Gone in 60 Seconds; The Hunted; Kidnap; Stolen; Taken; The Transporter; Wheelman*

Classic films: *Duel; The Fugitive; The Gauntlet; The Getaway; North by Northwest; The Running Man; Speed*

Subgenre: Superhero

Contemporary films: *The Amazing Spider-Man; Ant-Man and the Wasp; Aquaman; Avengers films; Batman Begins; Black Panther; Daredevil; The Dark Knight; Deadpool; Fantastic 4; Guardians of the Galaxy; Hancock; Hellboy; The Incredible Hulk; The Incredibles; Iron Man; Justice League; Logan; Teenage Mutant Ninja Turtles; Thor; Thor: Ragnarok; Watchmen; Wonder Woman; X-Men*

Classic films: *Batman; The Crow; Darkman; Mystery Men; The Phantom; Spawn; Supergirl; Superman*

Subgenre: Martial arts

Contemporary films: *Crouching Tiger, Hidden Dragon; Fearless; Fists of Legend; The Grandmaster; Hero; House of Flying Daggers; IP Man; Kiss of the Dragon; The Man with the Iron Fists; Power Rangers; The Protector; The Raid; Shaolin; True Legend; Unleashed*

Classic films: *Any Jackie Chan or Bruce Lee Movie; Beverly Hills Ninja; Fist of Legend films; Iron Monkey; The Legend; Once Upon a Time in China; Shogun Assassin*

Subgenre: Western

Contemporary films: *The Alamo; Appaloosa; The Assassination of Jesse James by the Coward Robert Ford; The Ballad of Lefty Brown; Brokeback Mountain; Django Unchained; Forsaken; Hickok; Hidalgo; Hostiles; Open Range; 3:10 to Yuma*

Classic films: *Butch Cassidy and the Sundance Kid; Dances with Wolves; High Noon; The Man Who Shot Liberty Valance; Once Upon a Time in the West; The Quick and the Dead; Red River; The Searchers; Shane; Silverado; Stagecoach; Tombstone; Unforgiven; Wild Bill; The Wild Bunch; Wyatt Earp; Young Guns*

Subgenre: Disaster

Contemporary films: *The Core; The Day After Tomorrow; Flood; Poseidon; 28 Days Later; 2012*

Classic films: *Airport; Armageddon; Avalanche; Dante's Peak; Deep Impact; Earthquake; Outbreak; The Poseidon Adventure; Titanic; The Towering Inferno*

GENRE: CRIME

Subgenre: Caper

Contemporary films: *The Bank Job; Confidence; Flawless; Gambit; The Good Thief; Heist; Inside Man; The Italian Job; The Ladykillers; Man on a Ledge; Ocean's Eleven Twelve Thirteen; The Score; Snatch; 3000 Miles to Graceland; Tower Heist*

Classic films: *The Brinks Job; Die Hard; The Great Train Robbery; How to Beat the High Cost of Living; Kelly's Heroes; The Silent Partner; The Sting; The Taking of Pelham One Two Three; The Thomas Crown Affair; Topkapi*

Subgenre: Detective/Mystery

Contemporary films: *From Hell; The Girl with the Dragon Tattoo; Insomnia; Kiss Kiss Bang Bang; Memento; Minority Report; Nightcrawler; Prisoners; Sherlock Holmes; Zodiac*

Classic films: *A Soldier's Story; Blade Runner; The Bone Collector; Chinatown; Gorky Park; The Maltese Falcon; The Name of the Rose; The Silence of the Lambs*

Subgenre: Prison

Contemporary films: *A Prayer Before Dawn; Brawl in Cell Block 99; Bronson; Chopper; Conviction; Escape Plan; The Escapist; Felon; Hunger; The Last Castle; Lockout; Maze*

Classic films: *Bad Boys; Birdman of Alcatraz; Brubaker; Cool Hand Luke; Dead Man Walking; Escape from Alcatraz; The Great Escape; The Green Mile; The Hurricane; In the Name of the Father; The Longest Yard; Midnight Express; Murder in the First; Papillion; The Shawshank Redemption*

Subgenre: Gangster

Contemporary films: *American Gangster; Cardboard Gangsters; City of God; The Departed; Eastern Promises; Gangs of New York; Gangster Land; Gotti; The Irishman; Once Upon a Time in Mexico; Sicario; Snatch*

Classic films: *Carlito's Way; Casino; Donnie Brasco; The Godfather;*

Goodfellas; Mean Streets; Miller's Crossing; Once Upon a Time in America; Prizzi's Honor; Scarface; The Untouchables

Subgenre: Police

Contemporary films: *The Black Dahlia; Brooklyn's Finest; Dark Blue; Departed; Hollywoodland; Miami Vice; Narc; Out of Time; Pride and Glory; Righteous Kill; Shaft; S.W.A.T.; Training Day*

Classic films: *Bad Lieutenant; Beverly Hills Cop; Colors; Cop Land; Dirty Harry; Fort Apache,The Bronx; 48 Hours; The French Connection; L.A. Confidential; Lethal Weapon; The New Centurions; The Onion Field; Serpico; The Untouchables*

Subgenre: Courtroom

Contemporary films: *American Violet; Conviction; Denial; Devil's Knot; Find Me Guilty; Hart's War; High Crimes; The Judge; The Lincoln Lawyer; North Country; Puncture; Runaway Jury*

Classic films: *A Civil Action; A Few Good Men; A Time To Kill; The Accused; And Justice for All; Amistad; Anatomy of a Murder; Class Action; The Client; Inherit the Wind; Judgment at Nuremberg; My Cousin Vinny; Philadelphia; Primal Fear; The Rainmaker; True Believer; 12 Angry Men; The Verdict; Witness for the Prosecution*

Subgenre: White collar

Contemporary films: *American Hustle; Boiler Room; Catch Me If You Can; Fun with Dick and Jane; Margin Call; Owning Mahowny; The Wolf of Wall Street*

Classic films: *Barbarians at the Gate; Class Action; The Hudsucker Proxy; The Insider; Quiz Show; Rogue Trader; Wall Street*

Subgenre: Youth gangs

Contemporary films: *City of God; Gangs of New York; Straight Outta Compton*

Classic films: *American History X; Boyz n the Hood; The Lords of Flatbush; The Outsiders; Rumble Fish; The Wanderers; The Warriors*

GENRE: THRILLER

Subgenre: Spy

Contemporary films: *Argo; Atomic Blonde; Body of Lies; The Bourne Identity Supremacy Ultimatum; Bridge of Spies; The Expendables;*

The Good Shepherd; James Bond films; Kingsman: The Secret
Service; Mission Impossible films; Munich; The Recruit; Red Sparrow;
Rendition; Salt; Spy Game; Tinker Tailor Soldier Spy; Zero Dark Thirty

Classic films: *Clear and Present Danger; The Conversation; The Falcon
and the Snowman; The Ipcress File; James Bond films; Marathon
Man; North by Northwest; Patriot Games; Ronin; Three Days of the
Condor*

Subgenre: Political

Contemporary films: *The Contender; The Ides of March; The
Interpreter; The Lives of Others; Snowden; State of Play; Vantage
Point*

Classic films: *All the President's Men; The Day of the Jackal; Enemy of
the State; Executive Action; JFK; The Manchurian Candidate; The
Parallax View; Winter Kills*

Subgenre: Conspiracy

Contemporary films: *Apollo 18; Changeling; The Conspiracy;
The Conspirator; The Da Vinci Code; Icarus; The Insider; The
International; Shutter Island; Syriana*

Classic films: *The Boys From Brazil; Capricorn One; The China
Syndrome; Conspiracy Theory; The Firm; The Net; The Pelican Brief;
Silkwood*

Subgenre: Suspense

Contemporary films: *All the Money in the World; Black Swan;
Flightplan; 47 Meters Down; Fracture; Gothika; Identity; Mother!;
Mr. Brooks; Panic Room; Phone Booth; Side Effects; Unforgettable*

Classic films: *A Perfect Murder; Arlington Road; Basic Instinct; Cape
Fear; Fatal Attraction; The Game; The Negotiator; Pacific Heights*

Subgenre: Revenge

Contemporary films: *The Foreigner; John Wick; Kill Bill; Law Abiding
Citizen; Machete; Man on Fire; Munich; Revenge; Three Billboards
Outside Ebbing, Missouri; True Grit; V for Vendetta*

Classic films: *Braveheart; Cape Fear; The Crow; Death Wish;
Desperado; Falling Down; Get Carter; Payback; Point Blank;
Sleepers; Straw Dogs*

GENRE: COMIC

Subgenre: Situation

Contemporary films: *Anchorman films; The Campaign; Daddy's Home; The Hangover; Horrible Bosses; The House; Meet the Parents films; Old School; Snatched; Ted; Tropic Thunder; We're the Millers*

Classic films: *Driving Miss Daisy; The Odd Couple; Tootsie*

Subgenre: Romantic

Contemporary films: *The Big Sick; Bridget Jones Baby; Crazy, Stupid, Love; Date Night; Everybody Loves Somebody; Forgetting Sarah Marshall; The 40-Year-Old Virgin; Friends with Benefits; The Girl Next Door; Home Again; How to be Single; The Incredible Jessica James; Knocked Up; The Late Bloomer; Paris Can Wait; The Perfect Match; Table 19; The Ugly Truth; Zack and Miri Make a Porno*

Classic films: *Annie Hall; As Good as It Gets; Pretty Woman; Sleepless in Seattle; When Harry Met Sally; You've Got Mail*

Subgenre: Buddy

Contemporary films: *Cop Out; Dude, Where's My Car?; Due Date; Harold & Kumar Go to White Castle; The Heat; Hot Fuzz; Get Him to the Greek; The Good Guys; The Guard; I Love You, Man; The Other Guys; Pineapple Express; Starsky & Hutch; Step Brothers; Superbad; 21/22 Jump Street; Wedding Crashers*

Classic films: *Dragnet; Dumb and Dumber; 48 Hours; The Last Boy Scout; Lethal Weapon; Loose Cannons; Men in Black; Midnight Run; Running Scared; Rush Hour; Spies Like Us; Stakeout; Stir Crazy; Turner & Hooch; Twins; White Men Can't Jump*

Subgenre: Parody

Contemporary films: *A Million Ways to Die in the West; Austin Powers in Goldmember; Black Dynamite; Kung Pow! Enter the Fist; MacGruber; Not Another Teen Movie; Scary Movie; Team America: World Police; Walk Hard: The Dewey Cox Story*

Classic films: *Airplane; Austin Powers films; Blazing Saddles; The Brady Bunch Movie; Fatal Instinct; Loaded Weapon; Murder by Death; Naked Gun; Robin Hood: Men in Tights; Spaceballs; This Is Spinal Tap; Top Secret!; Young Frankenstein*

Subgenre: Satire

Contemporary films: *Borat; Bruno; The Death of Stalin; The Dictator; Idiocracy; In the Loop; The Interview; Thank You for Smoking; Zoolander*

Classic films: *Being There; Bob Roberts; Bulworth; Dr. Strangelove; Life of Brian; Network; The Ruling Class; Wag the Dog*

Subgenre: Farce

Contemporary films: *Burn After Reading; The Producers*

Classic films: *A Fish Called Wanda; A Funny Thing Happened on the Way to the Forum; Blame It on the Bellboy; The Imposters; It's a Mad, Mad, Mad, Mad World; Noises Off; The Party; The Pink Panther; Soapdish; Some Like It Hot*

Subgenre: Dark

Contemporary films: *Bad Teacher; Bad Santa; Death to Smoochy; Four Lions; I Don't Feel at Home in This World Anymore; In Bruges; Intolerable Cruelty; Little Miss Sunshine; Mary and Max; Seven Psychopaths; Shaun of the Dead; Sightseers; Snatch; This Is the End; Tucker and Dale vs. Evil; Visioneers; Zombieland*

Classic films: *A Clockwork Orange; After Hours; Barton Fink; The Big Lebowski; The Cable Guy; Death Becomes Her; Election; Fargo; Fear and Loathing in Las Vegas; Harold and Maude; Heathers; Ruthless People; Throw Momma from the Train; To Die For; The War of the Roses; What About Bob?*

Subgenre: Camp

Contemporary films: *O Brother Where Art Thou?; Bubba Ho-Tep; Catwoman; The Grand Budapest Hotel; Hairspray; Sharknado; Snakes on a Plane*

Classic films: *Ace Ventura; The Adventures of Priscilla, Queen of the Desert; The Birdcage; Little Shop of Horrors; Pink Flamingos; Polyester; The Rocky Horror Picture Show; Strictly Ballroom*

Genre: Romance

Contemporary films: *A Good Year; Brooklyn; Call Me by Your Name; Disobedience; Everybody Loves Somebody; Film Stars Don't Die in Liverpool; The Holiday; Love, Actually; Lovely, Still; Made of Honor; Maid in Manhattan; Must Love Dogs; Nights in Rodanthe; The*

Notebook; Phantom Thread; Pride and Prejudice; The Proposal; The Secret; Under the Tuscan Sun; The Vow; Waitress

Classic films: Annie Hall; Dr. Zhivago; Ghost; Jane Eyre; Love Story; Moonstruck; Notting Hill; Pretty Woman; Say Anything; Sleepless in Seattle; Tess; When Harry Met Sally; You've Got Mail

GENRE: MUSICAL

Contemporary films: A Star Is Born; Across the Universe; Anna and the Apocalypse; Chicago; Coco; Dreamgirls; The Greatest Showman; Hairspray; Into the Woods; Jersey Boys; Les Misérables; Mamma Mia!; Mary Poppins Returns; Moulin Rouge; The Phantom of the Opera; The Producers; Rock of Ages; Straight Outta Compton; Sweeney Todd: The Demon Barber of Fleet Street

Classic films: A Chorus Line; All That Jazz; Annie; Beauty and the Beast; The Best Little Whorehouse in Texas; Evita; Fame; Funny Girl; Grease; The Lion King; Little Shop of Horrors; Newsies; The Pirates of Penzance; Yentl

GENRE: COMPETITION

Contemporary films: Ali; Battle of the Sexes; Bend It Like Beckham; Bleed for This; Borg vs. McEnroe; Bring It On; Cinderella Man; Eddie the Eagle; The Fighter; 42; Friday Night Lights; Goon; The Greatest Game Ever Played; The Hunger Games; Hands of Stone; I, Tonya; Invictus; Invincible; Jawbone; The Legend of Bagger Vance; McFarland, USA; Miracle; Moneyball; Pitch Perfect; Queen of Katwe; Real Steel; Remember the Titans; Rush; Seabiscuit; Southpaw; Warrior; Whip It; Wimbledon

Classic films: A League of Their Own; Any Given Sunday; The Big Blue; Bull Durham; Days of Thunder; Chariots of Fire; The Color of Money; Hoosiers; The Hustler; The Longest Yard; North Dallas Forty; Rocky; Searching for Bobby Fisher; Slap Shot; They Shoot Horses, Don't They?; Tin Cup

GENRE: INSPIRATIONAL

Contemporary films: A Beautiful Mind; Breathe; The Diving Bell and the Butterfly; Door to Door; I Am Sam; Infinitely Polar Bear; The Intouchables; Lars and the Real Girl; Margarita with a Straw; Marie's Story; The King's Speech; Ray; The Sessions; The Soloist; Still Alice; The Theory of Everything; 23 Blast

Classic films: *Awakenings; Bang the Drum Slowly; Brian's Song; Charly; Children of a Lesser God; The Elephant Man; Forrest Gump; Girl, Interrupted; Ice Castles; Mask; The Miracle Worker; My Left Foot; Philadelphia; Rain Man; Shine*

GENRE: ROAD PICTURE

Contemporary films: *About Schmidt; The Darjeeling Limited; EuroTrip; The Guilt Trip; Into the Wild; Little Miss Sunshine; The Motorcycle Diaries; Nebraska; O Brother Where Art Thou?;On the Road; One Week; Road Trip; Sideways; The Trip*

Classic films: *Duel; Dumb and Dumber; Easy Rider; It Happened One Night; The Journey of Natty Gann; Planes, Trains and Automobiles; Rain Man; The Silver Streak; The Straight Story; Thelma & Louise*

GENRE: ANIMAL/WILDLIFE

Contemporary films: *A Dog's Purpose; Because of Winn-Dixie; Beverly Hills Chihuahua; Big Miracle; Charlotte's Web; Dolphin Tale; Eight Below; Hidalgo; Isle of Dogs; Lassie; Life of Pi; Marmaduke; Max; War Horse*

Classic films: *The Adventures of Milo and Otis; Air Bud; Andre; Babe; The Bear; Beethoven; The Black Stallion; Dunston Checks In; Free Willy; The Incredible Journey; Mighty Joe Young; Never Cry Wolf; Old Yeller; 101 Dalmatians*

GENRE: BIOGRAPHY

Contemporary films: *Ali; American Splendor; American Sniper; The Aviator; Beautiful Boy; Black Mass; Bohemian Rhapsody; Boy Erased; Capote; The Disaster Artist; First Man; Florence Foster Jenkins; Foxcatcher; Frida; Genius Team; Hidden Figures; Hitchcock; The Iron Lady; J. Edgar; Julie and Julia; The Last King of Scotland; La Vie en Rose; Lincoln; Marshall; Milk; Monster; Paterno; The Queen; Ray; Snowden; Steve Jobs; Sully; Thank You for Your Service; The Theory of Everything; Trumbo; Walk the Line; Whiskey Tango Foxtrot*

Classic films: *Bird; Chaplin; Coal Miner's Daughter; The Doors; Ed Wood; Elizabeth; Gandhi; Lady Sings the Blues; The Last Emperor; Lenny; Man on the Moon; Patton; Raging Bull*

GENRE: PERIOD PIECE

Contemporary films: *Alexander; Anna Karenina; Atonement; Becoming Jane; The Count of Monte Cristo; The Duchess; The Four Feathers; Gangs of New York; Girl with a Pearl Earring; Gladiator; Gosford Park; Victoria; The Importance of Being Earnest; Jane Eyre; King Arthur; Kingdom of Heaven; The Last Samurai; The Libertine; Marie Antoinette; Memoirs of a Geisha; The Merchant of Venice; The New World; Nicholas Nickelby; The Other Boleyn Girl; The Painted Veil; Pride and Prejudice; Quills; Troy; Tulip Fever; Vanity Fair; Victoria & Abdul*

Classic films: *A Room with a View; The Age of Innocence; Ben-Hur; Brideshead Revisited; The Crucible; Dangerous Liaisons; Elizabeth; Emma; Glory; Hamlet; The Last of the Mohicans; Little Women; Mansfield Park; Much Ado About Nothing; Onegin; The Piano; The Portrait of a Lady; The Remains of the Day; Restoration; Sense and Sensibility; Shakespeare in Love; Spartacus; Valmont; Wuthering Heights*

GENRE: RITE OF PASSAGE / COMING OF AGE

Contemporary films: *Adventureland; Almost Famous; An Education; Boyhood; The Edge of Seventeen; Garden State; Girlhood; Juno; The Kite Runner; Mean Girls; Moonrise Kingdom; Never Let Me Go; The Perks of Being a Wallflower; The Sisterhood of the Traveling Pants; The Spectacular Now; The Squid and the Whale; Submarine; Superbad; Thirteen; The Way Way Back; Whale Rider*

Classic films: *American Graffiti; Boyz n the Hood; Breaking Away; The Chosen; Dazed and Confused; Dead Poets Society; Diner; Fast Times at Ridgemont High; The Graduate; The Last Picture Show; Mystic Pizza; My American Cousin; My Life as a Dog; Risky Business; Rushmore; The Sandlot; Sixteen Candles; Stand by Me; Summer of '42; This Boy's Life*

GENRE: RAGS TO RICHES

Contemporary films: *The Artist; Boiler Room; The Founder; Get Rich or Die Tryin'; Jersey Boys; Joy; Maid in Manhattan; Notorious; One Chance; The Pursuit of Happyness; Ray; Slumdog Millionaire; Straight Outta Compton; There Will Be Blood; The Wolf of Wall Street*

Classic films: *Cinderella; Citizen Kane; Coal Miner's Daughter; Funny Girl; The Hudsucker Proxy; Little Voice; My Fair Lady; Pretty Woman; Ragtime; Working Girl*

GENRE: SOCIAL ISSUES

Contemporary films: *Blackkklansman; Crash; Dallas Buyers Club; Fruitvale Station; The Life of David Gale; Loving; Mandela: Long Walk to Freedom; Maria Full of Grace; Milk; Selma; Tomboy; Traffic; 12 Years a Slave; Water*

Classic films : And the Band Played On; Baby Boom; Dead Man Walking; Do the Right Thing; The Grapes of Wrath; Guess Who's Coming to Dinner; The Long Walk Home; Matewan; Mississippi Burning; 9 to 5; Norma Rae; Philadelphia; Ticket to Heaven

---

Debate is good

As noted, a lot of these films are hybrids, meaning they're a combination of more than one genre. My rule in terms of classification of hybrid films is to determine which genre has primacy. You may disagree with some of my classifications. Debate is good!

\\\

Conventions vs. Clichés

Conventions are certain actions, plots, archetypes, or other story elements that are endemic to particular genres. They're important to identify because they've evolved over time and, for creative reasons, they work well for their genres.

Watch and borrow

If you're going to work in multiple genres, it's a good idea to become familiar with each of their conventions. For instance, if you're writing a pirate movie or a disaster movie or a romance, spend some time watching films in these genres. Identify their conventions and use them to shorten your writing process by not having to reinvent the wheel.

Bad laughs

Some genre conventions have become **clichés** because they've been used by writers so many times they now call attention to themselves, which can pull the audience out of the story. Sometimes they even evoke **bad laughs**, where the audience is laughing at you, not with you. This is death for a writer, unless you intend to write a "bad funny" movie, such as *Airplane*, which mined every airplane disaster movie cliché for comic gold.

Caper conventions

In many caper films, it's a convention that the rich "victim" of the caper (it could be an individual or an institution) is venal or criminal in some way, meaning that the caper, if successful, will have these creeps receive their just desserts, engendering sympathy for the thieves.

Here's another caper convention: the protagonist pulls off the caper and it looks like they're going to get away scot free with the loot. Then something unexpected (and ironic) happens, and while they may not get caught, they lose all the loot they just stole.

With this caper convention, *no one* gets the loot. It either ends up at the bottom of the sea or scatters to the wind or is burned up in a fire. Ultimately it doesn't matter, because in pulling off the caper, the protagonist has realized their personal goal. In fact, often they smile, shake their head (i.e., "easy come, easy go") and walk off into the sunset.

Do you recognize this caper convention? Why do you think it evolved? I think it's because ultimately—as in the above example—it's not the success of the caper that's the true measure of success for the protagonist, so the loot itself is expendable.

A horror convention

Another common example of a genre convention is the **false ending**. Horror stories seem to resolve and we think everything is done, but of course the monster suddenly pops up again and has to get bopped one last time before it's dispatched once and for all.

One of the most famous false endings occurs in the original *Alien* movie when Ripley gets into the shuttle and launches from the *Nostromo* just before it self-destructs. We think the alien was destroyed in the blast; however, it has hidden itself away on the shuttle and Ripley must use her wits and gumption to destroy it once and for all.

EXAMPLES OF
GENRE CONVENTIONS

CAPER MOVIE CONVENTIONS
- **The job to end all jobs:** The caper is either the protagonist's biggest score ever and/or it is their last job before they retire
- **Assembly of team members:** Each member has a specific area of expertise, which is critical to pulling off the caper
- **Planning:** The plan is laid out with precision; sometimes there are practice runs
- **Plan goes awry:** Something unanticipated goes wrong and the team is forced to improvise
- **Twist ending:** A surprise reveal and/or outcome at the end of the story

HORROR MOVIE CONVENTIONS
- **Isolation:** Outside help is unavailable, so victims must fend for themselves
- **Innocent and/or virginal victims:** Stacks the odds in favor of the evil and more worldly antagonist

- **Inclement weather:** Provides atmosphere and also traps the victims in their location
- **Paranoia:** Everyone is suspect and everything is a potential threat
- **False scares:** Startling threats that turn out to be benign, but still scare the bejeezus out of us
- **False ending:** The antagonist appears to be defeated, but then unexpectedly rises up for one final assault

WAR MOVIE CONVENTIONS

- **Impossible/suicide mission:** The odds of success are low or nil
- **Ragtag, burnt out unit:** Battle-weary soldiers may not be able to execute the mission
- **Green commanding officer:** Lack of experience creates conflict with veteran soldiers under his/her command
- **Insufficient supplies and/or broken or jury-rigged gear:** The unit lacks the weapons and gear necessary for success, forcing them to improvise
- **Intelligence failure:** The enemy is not where they're supposed to be
- **Sacrifice:** Unit suffers casualties, loses critical personnel
- **Heroism:** The least likely member performs the bravest feat

Clichés

Every genre has its conventions and, as screenwriters, our challenge is to figure out a fresh take so that audiences won't recognize them as hoary clichés that they've seen a thousand times before. For fun, following is a collection of my top 100 movie clichés. Enjoy!

100 THINGS YOU WOULD
NEVER KNOW WITHOUT THE MOVIES

1. During all police investigations, it will be necessary to visit a strip joint at least once.

2. If being chased through the city, you can usually take cover in a passing St. Patrick's Day parade—at any time of the year.

3. The ventilation system of any building is the ideal hiding place. No one will ever think of looking for you in there, and you can crawl to any other part of the building.

4. You're likely to survive any battle in any war unless you make the mistake of showing someone a photo of your sweetheart back home.

5. If your resort town is threatened by an imminent natural disaster or killer beast, the mayor's first concern will be tourism.

6. All single women own a cat.

7. A man will show no pain while taking the most hellacious beating, but will wince like a baby when a woman tries to clean his wounds.

8. When paying for a taxicab, don't look at your wallet as you take out a bill. Just grab one at random. It will always be the exact fare.

9. Loft-style apartments in New York City are well within the means of most people—whether they're employed or not.

10. Kitchens don't have light switches. When entering at night, you should open the refrigerator and use that light instead.

11. Mothers routinely cook eggs, bacon, and waffles every morning, even though their husband and children never have time to eat them.

12. If you find yourself in a misunderstanding that could be cleared up with a simple explanation, for goodness sake, keep your mouth shut.

13. The chief of police will always suspend their star detective—or will give them forty-eight hours to solve the case.

14. If a killer is hiding in your house, it's easy to find him. Just run a bath—even if it's in the middle of the afternoon—then look in the mirror and he'll be behind you.

15. A person being pursued will always stop to throw something at the person chasing them—even though it take three times longer to throw the obstacles than it does for the pursuer to jump over them.

16. A cough is invariably a sign of terminal illness.

17. It's always possible to park directly in front of the building you're visiting.

18. At least one in a pair of identical twins is always born evil.

19. When confronted by an international terrorist, wisecracks are your best weapon.

20. One man shooting twenty men has a better chance of killing them than twenty men firing at the same man.

21. A gang of terrorists will always separate and search for an intruder on their own, so they can be picked off one by one.

22. Megalomaniacs bent on world domination can't resist telling their arch nemesis every detail of their evil plan.

23. A huge full moon can occur for several nights in a row.

24. If the person you are chasing has just taken the elevator down from the twentieth floor, you'll be able to get to the street quicker by running down the stairs.

25. Most people keep a collection of newspaper clippings— especially if any of their family or friends have died in a strange boating accident.

26. It doesn't matter if you're outnumbered in a fight involving martial arts—your enemies will wait patiently to attack you one by one by dancing around in a threatening manner until you have dispatched their predecessors.

27. Dogs always know who's bad and will growl and bark at them.

28. When someone is knocked unconscious by a blow to the head, they'll never suffer a concussion or brain damage.

29. The most gorgeous girl in high school or college will never be able to get a date.

30. If you suddenly think there's an intruder in your house, your cat will choose that precise moment to leap out at you from inside a cupboard.

31. Police departments give their officers personality tests to make sure they're assigned to a partner who's their total opposite.

32. When they're alone, all foreigners prefer to speak English to each other.

33. If there's a deranged killer on the loose, it will also coincide with a thunderstorm that has destroyed all the power and phone lines in the vicinity.

34. Any door lock can be picked by a credit card or paper clip in seconds—unless it's the door to a building on fire with a child trapped inside.

35. While teaching, teachers will always be interrupted mid-sentence by the end-of-class bell.

36. You can tell if a man is British because he'll be wearing a bow tie.

37. Radiation causes horrifying mutations—not to your future children, but to you, right there and then.

38. Sexy strippers with a heart of gold can operate most heavy machinery.

39. Rather than wasting bullets, megalomaniacs prefer to use complicated machinery involving fuses, pulley systems, deadly gases, lasers, and hungry sharks that will allow their captives enough time to escape.

40. The more a man and woman dislike each other, the more likely they'll fall in love.

41. Having any kind of job will make all fathers forget their son's eighth birthday.

42. Breaking news bulletins on TV usually feature a story that affects the main characters at that precise moment.

43. When first seen, all movie bartenders will be wiping a glass with a cloth.

44. In technology movies, a small, dingy, cluttered lab and eccentric techies equal high principles. Large, well-lit facilities mask sinister motives.

45. When you're climbing the outside of a tall building, gravity grows greater, causing your firearm to fall from your grasp, just when you need it most. You then waste precious time watching it fall to the ground, despite your immediate peril.

46. No matter how well foreigners speak English, they never master the word "yes" and will be forced to rely on saying it in their native tongue.

47. The bad guy has you in his sights, but he shouts your name before firing, allowing you to spin around and fire first.

48. Little girls who wear eyeglasses in movies always tell the truth. Little boys who wear eyeglasses in movies always lie.

49. If a woman steals clothes, the clothing, if a male's, will be too big. If a female's, the clothes will be skimpy and revealing.

50. If you're introduced as a recovering alcoholic who has been sober for an extended period of time, you'll fall off the wagon later in the film.

51. Just being a computer programmer means you know all backdoors to any kind of software on any kind of computer in any critical moment.

52. Women can run well in whatever footwear they're wearing.

53. The FBI team always arrives by helicopter, irrespective of where they came from.

54. In a horror film, if a person is advised against taking any action, they then do that exact thing.

55. The brawniest solider will die first and the stupidest officer will usually survive.

56. Automatic weapons are useless when confronted by a single-shot pistol.

57. Stolen vehicles are always fully fuelled and handle like muscle cars.

58. The protagonist must have a weird friend who's a social outcast.

59. Bullets fired inside an aircraft cabin always cause explosive decompression.

60. Precocious young kids are always smarter than their adult parents.

61. Summer camps are populated by the musically gifted and psychopaths.

62. Remote places of the world contain heretofore unknown giant versions of animals.

63. If a person knocks another out and steals their uniform, it will always fit perfectly, irrespective of the relative size, sex, or even species.

64. Anything alien that turns up on our planet uninvited is invariably out to kill us all.

65. If a horse encounters a rattlesnake, it will throw the rider off directly in the snake's direction.

66. Girls named after fruit—like Peaches or Cherry—are easy.

67. Zombies are deceptively speedy walkers.

68. Reading any book of spells aloud usually has catastrophic consequences.

69. Mobile phones work pretty much anywhere unless it's important that they do.

70. As people fall from high buildings, they always look back up at where they fell from.

71. In any fight between two combatants, the one with the least practical weapon will win.

72. Asking the question, "Do you think we'll get out of this?" never elicits an honest reply.

73. An onstage performer can instantly spot a loved one in a crowd of 20,000 people.

74. A soldier carrying a memento of a loved one, such as a jewelry or a photograph, has no chance of returning alive.

75. Fifty percent of henchmen are completely mute.

76. High schools always have a socially inept pariah who's secretly talented.

77. People who don't know their ancestry turn out to be very rich and/or descended from aristocracy.

78. When an email arrives, the computer screen animates with a huge envelope opening.

79. All dangerous expeditions must be led by a grizzled, experienced guide with a facial scar who dies horribly before the end.

80. In a two cop partnership, only one of them can be streetwise, own a cool car, or have a family.

81. A theater can only be saved from demolition by staging an expensive and complex musical on very short notice.

82. Every small town has a bitter and twisted individual whose sporting career was cut short by an unfortunate accident.

83. Falling from the roof of a moving train is much more likely to happen when the train crosses a high trestle bridge with a river below.

84. A dam has one purpose: to break.

85. A man will do more for a woman who has divorced him than for any other woman.

86. Explosive decompression on a plane will cause the overhead bins to fall open and disgorge reams of loose papers.

87. Victorian street urchins don't own shoes, but they all have some kind of hat.

88. People who are marooned on desert islands soon learn to make almost anything from bamboo.

89. People who retire always buy a boat with a cabin.

90. In a mountain climbing expedition, those afraid of heights will generally survive, but those who are confident and experienced will plummet to their deaths.

91. People falling from high buildings always pancake on the roof of a car.

92. All government agencies have computer software in which their logo is a prominent feature.

93. All explosive devices have a handy visual countdown timer and a redundant mechanism to fool anyone trying to defuse them.

94. Hand grenades always have plenty of time to explode, even if the idea is to throw them just before they go off.

95. When the protagonist destroys something in a spectacular explosion, he's either walking or driving away looking in the opposite direction.

96. Men who have been wrongly imprisoned never have anyone pick them up on the day they're released.

97. Bank tellers always telegraph their intent to press the panic button by glancing repeatedly at it until the bank robber threatens them not to press it.

98. All funerals are secretly attended by the person responsible for the death.

99. Female abductees always try to be nice to their kidnapper, but then get angry and tell them that their boyfriend/brother/father will kill them when they arrive.

100. A person waking up disoriented from a nightmare will only have awakened in reality about ten percent of the time. Usually they're still having the nightmare.

Mea culpa!

In the spirit of full disclosure, I must confess that in the films and television programs I've written or produced, I've "committed" numbers 17, 28, 40, 69, 74, 82 and 88.

None of us are immune!

14

§§§§§§§§§§§§§§§§§§§§§§§§§§§§§

Tone and Ground Rules

Tone can be described as the "story sensibility." It's how you as the writer want things to be played by the actors. For example, in drama, the tone is realistic. In melodrama, the tone is exaggerated and over-wrought. When in real life we admonish someone to "stop being so melodramatic," we're telling them to tone it down. To be real. There's a clear and understood difference.

Not only is it important as a writer to be clear about how you want your material to be played by the actors, it's important to do it from the very outset of the story.

Equally important is to "set the **ground rules**." Again in real life, we know that before playing a game, everyone has to understand the rules, or else it's chaos. It's the same within a story. So in addition to tone, we also have to establish the logic parameters—especially in speculative genres like science fiction.

The world in science fiction usually differs significantly from the world we know today. So in post-apocalyptic movies such as the *Mad Max* series, we need to know as soon as possible that this is a world where fuel and water are more valuable than gold. This logic will inform the rest of the film, so it's critical to show the audience how the world of the film works as quickly as possible.

A more recent example is the film *A Quiet Place*, where we learn almost immediately that the world has been invaded by blind, carnivorous aliens equipped with acute, bat-like hearing. The only way to survive is to not make a peep.

Logic violations are when the audience catches the writer departing from the established ground rules, which will cause a Parking Lot Test failure. Tone violations are similar in the sense that the audience will notice if the writer is mixing tones. Having established the ground rules at the start of the story, it's crucial that the tone remains consistent throughout.

A cautionary tale

Many years ago I cowrote and produced the comic film *Freezer Burn: The Invasion of Laxdale,* starring Tom Green and Crispin Glover. In the film, the villains are humanoid aliens who infiltrate a prairie town while posing as Dutch oil company executives falsely promising the townsfolk full employment and high-paying jobs.

Their real agenda is to heat up the planet to make Earth into an alien luxury resort and enslave humankind to serve as their chambermaids and cabana boys. While admittedly it was a goofy idea, the story was also a **cautionary tale** about greed and global warming.

Our protagonist, played by Green, was an embittered small town fallen sports hero (see cliché #82), who slowly cottons onto the conspiracy. All his scenes were played fairly straight, as the plot was so wacky, we thought he shouldn't be some kind of goofball.

On the other hand, because our townsfolk were so blinded by greed, we thought it would be funny to play the aliens as transparent villains. So our bad guys wore black suits and black hats, and the chief alien, played by Glover, spoke in angry, guttural alien-speak.

This was a tone choice. Instead of creating three-dimensional villains, we went "over-the-top" and had our baddies be overtly evil. However, upon release, the film earned lukewarm reviews. When we conducted a postmortem, we realized that we had mixed tones. We had failed to keep the same silliness in the scenes that didn't involve the alien characters. So the lesson of this chapter (and maybe of my career) is: *don't mix tones*. If you do, the audience will start wondering which film they're watching.

Permission to laugh

Permission to laugh is another aspect of setting the ground rules. In a comic film, the audience must be given permission to laugh, which means not only do we have to make the tone clear (i.e., the "kind" of funny) but we also have to get to the first laugh quickly. If not, the audience will be unsure when or even *if* they should laugh going forward.

A case in point: black comedies are stories in which the screenwriter makes us laugh at things that would normally horrify us. If the tone of this type of humor isn't set up and the audience given permission to laugh, the audience might actually *be* horrified.

An example can be found in the darkly comic film *Mystery Men*. Remember the scene where our intrepid heroes try to rescue the egotistical and vain Captain Amazing from Casanova Frankenstein's doomsday machine?

Unsure how the contraption works, they flip the wrong lever and accidentally electrocute Captain Amazing to a crisp. It's hilarious! Had we not been given permission to laugh and had the dark comic tone not been clearly established, we could have been aghast.

Summary

So to review, it's important to 1) set the tone and ground rules clearly from the earliest possible moment and then 2) maintain the same tone consistently throughout the story and be careful not to violate any of the ground rules that you've established.

\\\\\\\\\\\\\\\\\\\\\\\\\\\\\\\\\\\\

Activity vs. Action

Activity is what in an earlier era might have been called "stage business." For us, it means movement without an underlying purpose. Activity is just something to occupy characters so they're not static. In a screenplay, activity is undesirable because it lacks intention. For example, a character unconsciously fidgeting with a pencil is activity.

Action, on the other hand, is activity with intention. The character isn't just doing something, they're doing it *to an end*. Their activity is *directed*. Because of this, we learn something about them while absorbing other information at the same time. So someone fidgeting with a pencil because they're *secretly telling a lie* is action. Poker players would call this a "tell."

Turning activity into action

Every activity has the potential to be an action. For instance, you write a simple scene of someone parking a car and entering a house, which is activity. For an audience, activity is boring. This pedestrian scene would likely end up on the cutting room floor.

But let's tweak the scene a bit. How is the car parked? Does the driver race into the driveway and slam on the brakes? Does the driver dash into the house with urgency? Or does the car approach slowly up the street, its headlights out, and then coast to a stop? Does the driver ease out, shut the car door with a click and tip-toe into the house?

In both cases, along with the activity of a car parking and the driver entering a house, there's *intention*. In the first case, the audience is wondering, what's the urgency? In the second case, they're wondering why the driver is skulking around. Without intention, the audience wouldn't care about someone getting out of a car and entering a house.

Aim for multilevel information

Sticking with this example, let's layer on more information by asking a few questions: what kind of car is it? A late model Audi? A beater with duct tape covering a broken taillight? A truck with a tradesman's ad on the side? A classic pink convertible with fins?

What if it's raining? Does the driver have an umbrella? If so, is it black or does it have a design or logo? Or, lacking an umbrella, do they cover their head with a newspaper? Or do they lean their head back and open their mouth to joyously swallow the rain?

These details tell us something about this person's social rank, sense of style, financial status, how they relate to their environment, state of mind. and so on. Every scene is an opportunity to integrate multiple levels of information.

Remember we want to be as efficient as possible in our scene descriptions. That same quest for efficiency extends to what unfolds onscreen. Every sentence has to provide multiple levels of information. And it should contain action, not just activity.

16

///////////////////////////////////////

Scene Structure

Often stuck writers will try to accomplish far too much in
scenes. These omnibus-type scenes should have ideally been
divided into separate, discrete scenes (assuming they're all
important to the narrative). So let's take a moment to define
a scene.

A **scene** is action that takes place in one area, which tradi-
tionally has been defined by a lighting setup. In other words,
each new lighting setup is a new scene. Even a shot where
the camera follows the actors from one place to another (e.g.,
inside to outside) would technically be one scene, since it's still
one lighting setup.

With CGI shots now bobbing and weaving in and out of
multiple locations, this definition of a scene may seem somewhat archaic. Nevertheless, it still applies on the written page,
regardless of whether the lighting is practical (on set) or digital
(computer generated).

Mini-screenplay

Every scene is like a mini-screenplay in that each has a beginning, middle, and end. The beginning of the scene often (but not always) follows a decision by a character to do an action, the middle is the action itself, and the end is the result of the action.

Answering to the premise

Each scene should answer in some way to the premise via three elements:

1. Idea: the action, that is, the scene itself
2. Function: how the scene relates to the first, second, or third word of the premise
3. Character: how the scene further reveals character

For example, imagine the following scene: We're in a bar in the old west. An intense young cowboy parts the swinging doors, strides up to the portly bartender and says, "I'm looking for the man who shot my pa." Sensing danger, the bartender raises his hands and slowly ducks down behind the bar.

Everyone else vacates the joint, except for a slick cardsharp who remains seated at a table, his cowboy hat low, silently scanning a poker hand. The young cowboy draws his gun and approaches the cardsharp, who reaches into his sleeve and reveals an ace.

A gunshot rings out and, struck in the back, the young cowboy falls dead. The bartender is standing behind him, brandishing a smoking shotgun. The cardsharp nods and tips his hat. The premise of this movie is "revenge kills innocence." Let's do the analysis:

1. Idea: the cardsharp outsmarts the young cowboy

2. Function: literally, the death of innocence

3. Character: the cardsharp has ice water in his veins

Winning the scene

Every scene has someone who wins, meaning it's "their" scene. Even in scenes where people make friends, one of them wins the scene—here it's the one who initiated the friendship. The character who wins the most scenes in a story is the protagonist. If your protagonist doesn't win the most scenes in your story, it may be why you're stuck.

Multilevel

Just as action should be **multilevel**, including more than one level of information, each scene should include secondary and tertiary information. If a perfunctory scene is required (packing clothes, driving somewhere), then other information should be integrated to enrich the scene, justifying its inclusion.

Rhythm

If possible, scenes should vary in **rhythm**, striking a balance between the long/short, day/night, interior/exterior, dialogue/non-dialogue, and so forth. Without ebb and flow and dynamic rhythm, the narrative will be flat and uniform.

Emotion

Crucially, each scene should be about an *emotion*. This is important because you want your audience to connect with your material on an emotional level. We used the example of the car pulling into the driveway and the driver entering the house. We had two ways of turning it from activity to action.

In the first scenario, the driver hurried into the house, and in the second scenario, the driver snuck inside.

So what's the emotion being felt by the driver in each scenario? The driver who hurried into the house was probably feeling fear or excitement about something that was about to happen or something that had just happened. The driver who snuck in the house might have been feeling malice or perhaps anxiety about being discovered.

Whichever emotion predominates, it's what the actor will play onscreen. And here's why this is important: if you as the writer are unclear about what the character is feeling, then when the scene is shot, the actor and/or director will impose their own interpretation.

This might result in a head-smacking moment when you view the completed scene and wonder, "What were they thinking?" Unfortunately, it won't be their fault; it will be *your* fault for not being clear on the page about how you wanted the scene played.

So in summary, when you write a scene, ask yourself what emotions the characters are feeling. Then be clear about them on the page in a visual way so that those tasked with interpreting your material will get it right when they play it for the camera.

Point of attack and point of departure

Where do you begin a scene and where do you end a scene? In a screenplay, these are called the **point of attack** and the **point of departure**. The answer is this: start the scene at the latest possible moment and end the scene at the earliest possible moment.

You might initially write a long scene. When you go back and revise with fresh eyes, use only the part of the scene that's required and discard the rest. A scene should build to a moment that accomplishes the scene, then CUT or DISSOLVE to the next scene.

The function of the scene should dictate the point of departure, meaning that when the action is completed, end the scene. As for the point of attack or point of departure, use entrances and exits sparingly. If characters enter or leave, there must be a reason beyond just activity.

How many times have you seen this happen: a scene is over, then someone gets up and leaves and the rest of the characters look at each other, trying to find something to do until the director yells "cut!" Did I mention this...also...kills...pace?

SAMPLE SCENE STRUCTURE ANALYSES

CONTEMPORARY FILMS

Ocean's Eleven

Location: Restaurant in the Bellagio Hotel

Point of attack: Tess (Julia Roberts) is waiting to have dinner with her boyfriend, casino owner Terry Benedict (Andy Garcia). A hand taps her on the shoulder, she turns, and frowns when she sees it's her ex-husband, Danny Ocean (George Clooney), who sits down, uninvited

Middle: Tess vents about how Danny let her down and broke her heart when he went to jail, while Danny tries to convince her to leave Benedict, whom he believes is bad news

Point of departure: Tess refuses to leave Benedict or reconcile with Danny. Danny departs, looking heartbroken

Action: Danny wants Tess to come back to him

Winner of scene: Tess

Subplot: Danny spars verbally with Terry Benedict when Terry arrives to have dinner with Tess. Benedict shuts him down

Emotion: Heartbreak

Arena: Las Vegas

Premise: Audacity wins hearts

Idea: Danny is concerned about Tess's welfare

Function: Danny's love for Tess might put the caper at risk

Character: Danny Ocean is a romantic

Whiplash

Location: The apartment of Andrew's father, Jim Neimann (Paul Reiser)

Point of attack: Mid-meal, Andrew's aunt asks him how his drumming is coming along, but she's not really interested in his answer, indicating that she doesn't think much of either his field or his accomplishments, making him quietly seethe

Middle: Fed up with his relatives marginalizing his career ambitions, Andrew insults his cousins, telling them that they're mediocre and they won't achieve any kind of greatness or fame

Point of departure: Jim challenges Andrew, humiliating his son in front of everyone, causing him to leave the dinner table in a huff

Action: Andrew loses his appetite

Winner of scene: Jim

Subplot: Andrew is rude to his relatives and they respond in kind

Emotion: Arrogance

Arena: Private music school

Premise: Unbridled ambition forces isolation

Idea: Andrew's father is concerned that his son is getting too big for his britches

Function: Andrew is setting himself up for a fall

Character: Andrew is immature

CLASSIC FILMS

Parenthood

Location: Karen's house

Point of attack: Upset, Karen (Mary Steenburgen) is flipping through nude photos of her teenage daughter Julie (Martha Plimpton)

Middle: Conflict between Karen and Julie

Point of departure: Julie decides to move out, and Karen immediately regrets what she said

Action: Karen confronts Julie, who decides to move out of the house

Winner of scene: Julie

Subplot: Julie's brother is apathetic

Emotion: Impotence

Arena: Suburbia

Premise: Acceptance fosters happiness

Idea: Karen finds nude photos and confronts Julie

Function: Karen's self-doubt over her ability as a parent increases

Character: Karen is a pushover

Terms of Endearment

Location: Supermarket checkout line

Point of attack: When the cashier asks for payment

Middle: Conflict between Emma (Debra Winger) and cashier

Point of departure: Sam (John Lithgow) covers the shortfall and scolds the cashier for being rude

Action: Emma is buying groceries and doesn't have enough money to pay the bill

Winner of scene: Emma

Subplots: One son is embarrassed; the other son is unselfish; Sam is romantically interested; the other shoppers are impatient

Emotion: Triumph

Arena: Suburbia

Premise: Love overcomes sorrow

Idea: Emma doesn't have enough money for the groceries

Function: To help establish Emma as being ripe for an affair with Sam

Character: How Emma reacts to the cashier ("we're all the same, you know") tells us who she is. She doesn't respond with anger

Openings

Broadly speaking, there are two types of openings: the **slow build** and the **fast break**. A slow build eases us into the story, usually over multiple scenes before the protagonist encounters the inciting incident, which launches the rising action.

A fast break drops us right into the middle of an action scene. This is often followed by a scene or scenes where we're brought "up to speed," after which the protagonist encounters the inciting incident, launching the rising action.

Which of these openings to use is best dictated by the genre of the story. A romance would have a slow build. An action flick would have a fast break. There's no hard and fast rule, however. Whatever works for the story is the correct choice.

Visual openings

While dialogue is okay, many of the strongest openings use no dialogue and rely on visuals to pull us into the story. The classic example of a non-dialogue opening is the "Dawn of Man" sequence in *2001: A Space Odyssey*, which depicts feuding prehistoric hominids who discover how to kill.

Opening credits

As the writer, you won't have much control over the placement of the opening credits. Still, if you're doing a fast break, you can indicate on the page that credits are to roll and be completed before the first FADE IN. With a slow build, you could indicate the credits are to appear over picture, which might be preferable due to its economy.

Hook the audience quickly

Whichever opening you choose, the audience must be hooked quickly into the story, either through action, or alternatively through the dashing of expectations. A good example of a slow build leading to a surprise is the opening credit sequence of *Harold and Maude.*

In a tracking shot, the camera moves slowly around the parlor of a posh mansion, following a young man wearing a suit and dress shoes. He puts on some music, pulls out a chair, and climbs up on it. We don't see him above the shoulders.

Suddenly, he kicks the chair over and we cut to a WIDE SHOT of young Harold dangling from a noose, choking. If this isn't shocking enough, when his mother enters the room and shows *no concern* about Harold's grisly suicide attempt, we're flummoxed.

Teasers

This is also an example of a **teaser**, which is an opening that raises the question: "What's going on?" The audience is immediately hooked. Be careful though. There's a fine line between teasing an audience deliciously and teasing them for too long to the point of frustration. I could use a "blue" analogy here, but hey, this is a G-rated book.

At any rate, whatever question you pose to the audience in a teaser should be answered quickly. In the above example, we quickly learn that Harold is always faking suicide to get attention, which accounts for his socialite mother's unexpectedly blasé reaction.

FILM EXAMPLES OF

SLOW-BUILD AND FAST-BREAK OPENINGS

CONTEMPORARY FILMS

Deadpool

Opening: Deadpool (Ryan Reynolds) takes a cab to the middle of a bridge, where he launches into an action-filled sequence where he confronts a gang of thugs and dispatches them in the goriest possible ways.

Type: Fast break

The 40-Year-Old Virgin

Opening: We watch Andy Stitzer's (Steve Carrell's) morning routine and everything about his life suggests he needs to get laid.

Type: Slow build

Gravity

Opening: There are seven full minutes of satellite maintenance and casual banter before the astronauts receive a radio transmission warning that a Russian satellite has incurred a missile strike.

Type: Slow build

Minority Report

Opening: We witness a disturbing double homicide through foggy, staccato imagery generated by the "pre-cogs."

Type: Fast break

Ocean's Eleven

Opening: Danny Ocean (George Clooney) faces the parole board to explain why he broke the law and to provide assurance that he won't return to a life of crime.

Type: Slow build

Passengers

Opening: A year elapses after Jim Preston (Chris Pratt) is awakened from his pod when—desperately lonely—he decides to awaken Aurora Lane (Jennifer Lawrence) from her pod.

Type: Slow build

Star Trek: Into Darkness

Opening: Kirk (Chris Pine) and McCoy (Karl Urban) are being chased by primitives trying to kill them, while Spock (Zachary Quinto) is lowered into a volcano in order to activate a device and save the alien planet.

Type: Fast break

Classic filmsCity Slickers

Opening: Mitch Robbins (Billy Crystal) and his two buddies, seeking to recapture their lost youth, partake in the running of the bulls in Pamplona, Spain.

Type: Fast break

The Player

Opening: In one of the longest continuous takes in cinema, we're introduced to the cynical players who inhabit the world of a major Hollywood studio.

Type: Slow build

Twister

Opening: We experience the raw power and destruction of the tornado that killed Jo Thornton's (Helen Hunt's) father, which led to her career as a storm chaser.

Type: Fast break

Entrances and introducing main characters

Central characters are usually introduced in the opening of the film, but sometimes there's a delay or interval before they're introduced. Either way, the details of their initial appearance should be chosen carefully. As in life, first impressions matter.

For example, in the opening sequence of *A Beautiful Mind*, John Nash attends the president's reception as a freshman at Princeton. We see he is an introvert, lacking any social graces and, in particular, tact. As he surveys objects and people, via his point of view we see that he finds patterns in random objects. At first, we think this aptitude is part of his mathematical genius, but later we'll learn that he suffers from waking hallucinations, which almost destroy his career.

Timing

If it serves the story to delay the introduction of the protagonist, then we should *want* to meet them by the time they appear. Maybe they've been spoken about by other characters, filling us with anticipation of their impending arrival. Or maybe we've received information about them in some other way that's similarly piqued our interest.

When they *do* arrive, depending on the story, they shouldn't just "show up." They should be given an appropriate entrance. A classic example of an entrance is someone in formal attire descending a grand staircase. If you have that kind of story, that would be perfectly appropriate.

In the opening of *Ex Machina*, Caleb, a computer programmer, learns that he's won a competition to spend a week with his employer, the brilliant and rich Nathan Bateman. En route, Caleb learns that Bateman owns a huge tract of land in Alaska and is a recluse who lives off the grid in a secure, ultra-modern facility. The more Caleb learns about Nathan, the more we're intrigued. Caleb finally meets Nathan, who's pummeling a punching bag, explaining that he's sweating out a hangover. For Caleb—and the audience—Nathan seems more like a Joe Six-Pack than the wealthy eccentric genius we were expecting, which is a dashing of expectations that helps pique our interest.

FILM EXAMPLES OF
ENTRANCES

CONTEMPORARY FILMS

The Diving Bell and the Butterfly

Entrance: Jean-Dominique Bauby (Mathieu Amalric) awakens in a hospital, having suffered a stroke. He suffers from "locked in" syndrome, in which he's completely aware, but can only blink one eye. Roughly thirty minutes into the film, he glimpses his distorted, frozen face in the mirror and we are at last fully introduced to him.

Type: Delayed

Pirates of the Caribbean: The Curse of the Black Pearl

Entrance: Pirate Captain Jack Sparrow (Johnny Depp) appears to be sailing confidently into port...until we pull back and see that he is literally on a sinking ship. He nonchalantly steps onto the pier just as top of the crow's nest disappears under water.

Type: Not Delayed

CLASSIC FILMS

A Clockwork Orange

Entrance: The camera begins on a closeup of Alex (Malcolm McDowell) looking menacing. We pull back to reveal the milk bar with its pornographic mannequins as he explains in a voiceover that he and his droogs are getting prepped for an evening of "the old ultra-violence."

Type: Not Delayed

Amadeus

Entrance: Court composer Salieri (F. Murray Abraham) has heard about Mozart's genius, and as he mingles among the royal court, he speculates which person might be Mozart. Peeking into a side room, he's shocked to see that Mozart (Tom Hulce) is a sophomoric brat.

Type: Delayed

Lawrence of Arabia

Entrance: Sherif Ali (Omar Sharif) appears as a black speck on the horizon riding on his horse at full speed toward T. E. Lawrence (Peter O'Toole) and his guide. Through the shimmering heat waves, he appears as if to be a mirage. When he finally draws within range, he shoots Lawrence's guide dead for using his tribe's well without permission. When he arrives and dismounts, he defends the shooting as a just act.

Type: Delayed

Saturday Night Fever

Entrance: Carrying a can of paint, peacock Tony Manero (John Travolta) walks down the street in Brooklyn, putting clothes on layaway, eating pizza slices, and trying to pick up girls.

Type: Not Delayed

18

//

Setups and Payoffs

A **setup** is a detail that will come into play at some point later
in the story. The **payoff** is the moment that it comes into play.
Does every story use setups and payoffs? Yes, but of course
some genres use more, such as detective mysteries, in which
multiple clues seeded throughout the narrative must ultimately
be resolved.

Words vs. pictures

Like most everything in the writing of motion pictures, setups
and payoffs are most effective when they're visual. It's more
likely that an audience will remember a visual setup than one
contained in a piece of dialogue, especially if the setup and
payoff are far apart in the narrative, such as something set up
in Act I that pays off in Act III.

Invisibility

A setup should never be spotlighted or obvious. It should be
invisible. The audience should register it subconsciously, but
never take conscious note of it. A setup won't be detected by

the audience if it's woven seamlessly into a piece of action or activity.

Here's an example. Someone lights a cigarette. The gold lighter is monogrammed, which is the setup. We see the monogram, but we don't attribute it any significance, other than indicating the owner is wealthy. In the story, the character suffers amnesia. The payoff is when the monogram becomes a clue to the character's identity.

Another way to have the audience unconsciously register a setup is to leave it onscreen in the background of a scene for a long time. An example might be a fire extinguisher hanging on a wall that a character later uses as a weapon, which is the payoff.

Or maybe the fire extinguisher is used as propellant, as in the film *Gravity*. The setup is earlier in the story when the astronauts use their backpack propulsion systems, showing how in zero gravity a propellant can be used to maneuver with a measure of control.

The Gun in the Drawer

The phrase "the **Gun in the Drawer**" (or alternatively, "the Bear on the Beach") is a setup in which, in order to build tension, the audience is furnished with information that's withheld from some or all of the onscreen characters.

This is called putting the audience in a "**superior position.**" Tension naturally arises as the audience watches the characters go about their business, completely unaware of the impending danger. The payoff is when the gun is used (or the bear pounces).

Incidentally, Gun in the Drawer should not be confused with a **Smoking Gun**, which is an incriminating piece of

evidence in a detective/mystery story that unequivocally confirms the guilt of the perpetrator of the crime.

Contrast

Not all setups and payoffs have to do with planting props or
providing specific information. They can be used simply for
the purpose of contrast by showing a person at first failing at
some endeavor or activity and then, later on, succeeding.

For example, in the film *Rocky*, Rocky Balboa initially can't
run up the front steps of the Philadelphia Museum of Art without being completely winded. After a training montage, the
payoff is when he dashes up the steps two at a time and raises
his fists triumphantly in the air, which became an iconic image
from the film (in fact, there's a statue of Rocky Balboa striking
this pose in front of the Philadelphia Art Museum).

Foreshadowing

Foreshadowing is not the same as a setup. It falls more in the
realm of symbolism where, in a figurative way, it provides a
subtle hint of future events and/or outcomes.

For example, you might have a *Great Gatsby*–type of plot in
which the protagonist wants to be accepted into high society,
but not being high-born, they're an outsider. The plot of the
story will show them trying to be accepted, but tragically,
they'll fail.

To foreshadow the plot, the film might open with the
protagonist hitchhiking by the side of the highway. A luxury
automobile approaches. It's filled with rich people dressed in
gowns and tuxedoes, drinking champagne and having a rol-
licking good time.

The protagonist watches the automobile approach and pass by, without anyone inside casting them a glance or acknowledging that they exist. The entourage continues on, leaving the protagonist standing at the side of the road, bitter yet resolute.

The action of this scene foreshadows what's to come in the story without overtly stating it. Being "passed by" by high-society types is symbolic of what is going to happen in the rest of the story. It's the plot in a nutshell. It's also high-level writing.

In another example, the beginning of *Butch Cassidy and the Sundance Kid* features a sepia-toned silent movie depicting the exploits of the two robbers. It really looks like an anachronism which, not coincidentally, is what the film is about: the bank robber era of Butch and Sundance is coming to an end and a new modern age is about to begin.

Deus ex machina

The Latin phrase *deus ex machina* is used to describe a plot point in which the very thing that the protagonist desperately requires suddenly appears and is available for use. Audiences feel cheated when this happens. It's mentioned again here because a *deus ex machina* can also be regarded as a payoff *without* a setup. Don't deus it!

~~~~~~

FILM EXAMPLES OF
SETUPS AND PAYOFFS

CONTEMPORARY FILMS

Ex Machina

Setup: Caleb (Domhnall Gleeson) is interviewing the android Ava (Alicia Vikander), and he asks her what she would like to do if she were free. She innocently says she would like to stand at a traffic intersection in a city and experience the hustle and bustle of people hurrying past.

Payoff: The last shot of the film is Ava standing at a traffic intersection in a city, only now we know that it is with ominous intentions. For humanity, it's likely the beginning of the end. We lose her in the crowd. FADE OUT.

Get Out

Setup: After Chris (Daniel Kaluuya) and Rose (Allison Williams) arrive at her parents' house and he's introduced to everyone, including the Black help, they all sit down to have afternoon tea. Rose's mother Missy (Catherine Keener), a therapist, stirs her tea and lightly taps her spoon against the teacup three times. At the time, it seems like an innocent gesture—perhaps a force of habit.

Payoff: Later that night, Chris is sneaking back inside the house after smoking a cigarette. Missy is up and asks him to join her in the home office. She gently scolds Chris for smoking, then gets him to talk about a traumatic event in his life. As he becomes emotional, she taps her teaspoon. Now hypnotized, Chris drops into the "sunken place."

I, Robot

Setup: Early in the story, Sonny the robot (Al Tudyk) sees Del Spooner (Will Smith) wink at someone. Curious, Sonny asks what it means. Spooner says a wink is a sign of mutual trust, but then says, cynically, that he doubts a robot will be able to understand such a concept.

Payoff: Later in the story, Spooner finds himself facing two identical robots, both claiming they're Sonny, but one of them is a lethal threat. Spooner must make a quick life-and-death decision. Just then, one of the robots winks, revealing that it is the real Sonny. Spooner quickly destroys the other robot.

The King's Speech

Setup: The film opens with Prince Albert (Colin Firth), known familiarly as "Bertie," having to give a speech at the closing ceremonies of the 1925 British Empire Exhibition. Because of his uncontrollable stammering, he's humiliated.

Payoff: The film closes with Bertie, the newly christened King George VI, giving an inspirational speech over the radio at the onset of World War II, having conquered his stammering through courage and perseverance.

Phantom Thread

Setup: Alma (Vicky Krieps) and the cook gather mushrooms, then return to the kitchen, where the cook warns Alma about the poisonous mushrooms and shows her the book with the illustrations that clearly identify them.

Payoff: Later, in a moment of anger, Alma consults the book, selects a poisonous mushroom, and grates some of it into the tea that she's preparing for her moody husband Reynolds (Daniel Day-Lewis).

CLASSIC FILMS

One Flew Over the Cuckoo's Nest

Setup: Angry that he and the other inmates in the asylum won't be allowed to watch the World Series on television, McMurphy (Jack Nicholson) bets the others that he can hurl a 400-pound marble island through a window and escape. The inmates watch him fail to lift the impossibly heavy object. Giving up, McMurphy says, "But I tried, didn't I? Goddamnit, at least I did that."

Payoff: McMurphy, who's now been lobotomized, is compassionately euthanized by Chief Bronden who, inspired by McMurphy's free spirit, picks up the 400-pound island, smashes it through the window, climbs out, and escapes the madhouse. The other inmates awaken, realize what's happened and cheer uproariously.

Raiders of the Lost Ark

Setup: In the opening sequence, after narrowly escaping the blow guns of the natives, Indy (Harrison Ford) finds a snake in the biplane and freaks out, saying he hates snakes.

Payoff: When Indy has to go down into the Well of Souls, he drops his torch down first, revealing that the floor is covered with poisonous asps. Freaked out, he says, "Snakes. Why did it have to be snakes?"

The Shawshank Redemption

Setup: The pin-up posters in Andy Dufresne's (Tim Robbins) cell change over the years: the first is Rita Hayworth, the next is Marilyn Monroe, and the third is Raquel Welch. We think they're just a cinematic device to show the passage of time.

Payoff: After Dufresne escapes, Warden Norton (Bob Gunton) angrily throws a rock, and it pierces the pin-up poster. They peel it back to reveal a tunnel. We now realize the posters were meant for another purpose entirely: to conceal Andy's tunnel, which took him decades to dig using only a rock hammer.

19

\\\

Exposition

Many stuck screenwriters are challenged to integrate exposition seamlessly into their narrative. Fortunately, there are many effective techniques to tackle this problem. Often the exposition is information about events that happened before the opening fade in. These comprise the **backstory** of the film.

Imperceptible

Like setups, exposition shouldn't call attention to itself. Wherever possible, it should be incorporated into action. When we become aware that we're being fed information by the writer, it yanks us out of the story. Exposition should be concealed or finessed.

For example, in *Passengers*, Jim Preston is awakened prematurely from suspended animation. He's groggy and disoriented, so the AI has to explain where he is, when it is, how he got here and why. The AI also lets us know that Jim has an engineering background, which explains later how he's able to invent various gizmos and fix machines.

Visual vs. dialogue

Character exposition is ideal when characters can reveal themselves in scenes with little or no dialogue, that is, through action. As we've explored earlier, showing is much more powerful than telling. Someone with a PhD could tell us they're highly educated or instead we could pan across multiple framed degrees on the wall of their office.

Use conflict

If exposition must be conveyed through dialogue rather than visually, then try to have the characters do it in the context of some kind of conflict, like during a disagreement. The audience will be focused on the emotion, so they won't perceive they're also being fed information. In the *Passengers* example above, Jim's groggy frustration creates a bit of conflict that helps to disguise the exposition being conveyed by the AI character.

Red herrings

All exposition has to pay off in some way or else it will become a "red herring." A **red herring** is a detail that *because of its inclusion* we think will be important in some way; however, it ends up being of no importance whatsoever. It will leave the audience dangling and will no doubt be mentioned during a Parking Lot Test.

Employing experts

Sometimes exposition is about educating the audience about a specific aspect of your arena. Perhaps there are some technical concepts the audience needs to understand, but to avoid a college lecture, there needs to be a technique to finesse this exposition. One way to do this is to have knowledgeable characters explain things to lay characters.

At the time *The China Syndrome* was released, the public knew little about nuclear power reactors, so it was important to bring audiences up to speed on how they work so that when things went wrong, people would know that the impact of a nuclear reactor breakdown would be near catastrophic.

To address this, early in the narrative, a TV news crew arrives to do a human interest piece on the Ventanna Nuclear Plant. The activity of the scene is the plant public relations man doing a walk-through, explaining the layout and workings of the plant.

However, the action of the scene is that the news crew is being misled about the safety of the plant. We also learn about the central characters. Kimberly Wells (Jane Fonda) is ambitious and keen to advance from puff piece assignments and her cameraman, Richard Adams (Michael Douglas), is a skeptic, suspicious about what they're being told.

Supporting characters are also introduced, such as plant foreman Jack Godell (Jack Lemmon), who will later figure prominently in the story when he discovers the facility is unsafe and he barricades himself inside the control room to try to alert the public.

A lot is going on in the sequence, yet we are blissfully unaware that we're being "exposed" (sorry, couldn't resist) to a lot of dry, technical information about the workings of a nuclear power plant. We're absorbing the data, but focused elsewhere.

Another example is *Jurassic Park*. The audience needs to know the science behind the cloning of dinosaurs from DNA. Instead of listening to a scientific lecture, the central characters hop on an amusement-park type of ride, complete with adorable animation, where everything is explained, as will happen when the park is opened to the public.

These two examples are similar, because in both cases the central characters are set up as lay people who don't have knowledge. So as they're exposed to the information—while other action is happening—we're exposed to it as well. We piggyback on their lesson.

Delayed exposition

Exposition is usually introduced early in the narrative; however, there are times when it serves the story to have some of it delayed. In such cases, the story is succeeding if the audience is asking questions that are eventually answered. This is called **delayed exposition**. However, if the questions are left unanswered...I smell a red herring!

FILM EXAMPLES OF
EXPOSITION

CONTEMPORARY FILMS

The Big Short

Scene: While Margot Robbie luxuriates in a bubble bath drinking champagne, she explains esoteric, sleazy Wall Street investment schemes as if to an idiot.

Exposition: While unorthodox, this idea was clever and could readily be justified because it was consistent with the "in your face" tone of the film.

I, Robot

Scene: Spooner (Will Smith) and Calvin (Bridget Moynahan) enter Hogenmiller's lab. Wary, Spooner draws his gun, but Calvin assures him that a robot can't harm a human and she cites the three Laws of Robotics.

Exposition: We learn that 1) a robot is forbidden to harm a human being; 2) a robot must obey an order as long as it doesn't conflict with the first law; and 3) a robot can defend itself as long as its action doesn't conflict with the first or second laws.

The Martian

Scene: Astronaut and botanist Mark Watney (Matt Damon) is stranded on Mars. He decides to record a personal voice log for the record.

Exposition: We learn the following: 1) he has no way to contact NASA; 2) it will take four years for a resupply mission; 3) the HAB is only designed to last thirty-one days; 4) if the oxygenator breaks, he'll suffocate; 5) if the water reclaimer breaks, he'll die of thirst; 6) if the HAB breaches, he'll implode; and 7) eventually he's going to run out of food. In sum, we're learning that the odds of his survival are slim.

Moneyball

Scene: Oakland A's general manager Billy Beane (Brad Pitt) hires economist Peter Brand (Jonah Hill) to help him build a winning team. On his first day on the job, Billy asks Peter to "walk him through the board."

Exposition: Peter explains his mathematical system for picking value players who are able to get on base, even via walks, increasing the overall team odds of winning ball games.

Nightcrawler

Scene: While negotiating the sale of stolen goods, hustler and small-time thief Louis Bloom (Jake Gyllenhaal) tries to apply for a legitimate job at a scrap metal yard, but is rebuffed.

Exposition: We learn that even though he's a thief, Bloom is a smooth talker, has ambition, is incredibly persistent, and quite intelligent.

Roman J. Israel, Esq.

Scene: With his law partner of twenty-six years in a vegetative state in a hospital, Roman (Denzel Washington) suddenly has to find a new job and is awkwardly interviewing with Maya (Carmen Ejogo), who's a volunteer leader at a civil rights advocacy group.

Exposition: As he lists his bonafides, we learn where Roman went to school, that he chose to fight for his principles over personal enrichment and that he's still an activist lawyer who's only doing criminal work to support his fight for progressive initiatives.

Zero Dark Thirty

Scene: Maya (Jessica Chastain), a CIA intelligence officer, is newly arrived from Washington to a black site in Pakistan, where her colleague Dan (Jason Clarke) is interrogating a detainee by waterboarding him.

Exposition: We learn that while she has a hard time watching the torture, Maya is prepared to condone whatever measures are necessary to gather information on al-Qaeda and Osama bin Laden.

CLASSIC FILMS

Butch Cassidy and the Sundance Kid

Scene: Sundance (Robert Redford) is winning a poker game. One of the players accuses him of cheating. Butch (Paul Newman) arrives and defuses the situation by letting everyone know who they are messing with and gets the disgruntled player to back down, humiliating him in the process.

Exposition: We learn about Sundance's reputation and proficiency as a gunfighter, and we also learn about Butch's unflappable proclivity for philosophy, glibness, and irony.

Chinatown

Scene: As part of his investigation, private detective J. J. Gittes (Jack Nicholson) attends a city council meeting at City Hall regarding potential water shortages and the need for the proposed Alto Vallejo Dam.

Exposition: We see the principled Hollis Mulwray (Darrell Zwerling) oppose the project for engineering reasons, which plants the seed of a motive for his murder, although Gittes is only investigating him for an alleged infidelity.

20

WWWWWWWWWWWWWWW

Dialogue
and Subtext

It's been said that "dialogue is the lie" because people rarely say
what they mean, except in moments of intense emotion, when
they might blurt out the truth. So **subtext** is what characters
are *actually* feeling or thinking, as opposed to what they're
saying aloud.

In *Catch Me If You Can*, it's Christmas Eve. Fugitive forger
Frank Abagnale has called Detective Carl Hanratty to taunt
him on the phone. They're jousting verbally when Hanratty
realizes aloud that Frank has no one else to call on Christmas
Eve. Upset by this exposure, Frank hangs up the phone. The
subtext of their conversation: Frank is lonely.

Conversely, in the film *A Few Good Men*, in a courtroom
scene Colonel Jessep says to Lieutenant Kaffee, "You can't
handle the truth!" and then confirms that indeed he ordered
the code red that resulted in the killing of PFC Santiago. Jessep
has lost control of his temper and become so unhinged that he
unwittingly tells the truth, sealing his fate.

Earlier, we talked about the difference between persona and character, where persona is the face we show to the world and character is who we truly are. Similarly, unless you have a character who's authentic, like a child, dialogue is usually a reflection of someone's persona, while subtext is an expression of who they really are.

Most people aren't tremendously self-aware and can't make a distinction between their persona and their character. The exception would be a character who's consciously lying in an attempt to deceive others. If desired, subtext can be used to convey their true intent.

While subtext can be conveyed via onscreen action, it can also be contained in dialogue, where what's being said is less important that what's left unsaid. Before we delve into subtext however, let's first spend a little time talking about the spoken word.

Talking heads

First, if you *must* use dialogue, try to avoid "**talking heads**"— that is, people who sit or stand and statically converse. Instead, give your characters action or activity as they talk, as long as it's organic to the content of the scene.

An example—perhaps now cliché – is the teenage couple who are just getting to know each other, but they're poor, so they park by the airport runway and lie on the hood of the car, talking about the future while watching aircraft pass overhead.

Poetry of the vernacular

How people talk is just as important as *what* they say. Dialogue is "**poetry of the vernacular,**" meaning that characters have their own idioms, vocabulary, and rhythm sourced in their origins, class, and education. This should be reflected in their dialogue.

Speech patterns can be just as revealing about a character as what they're saying. Characters shouldn't all have the same voice, otherwise we'll feel the writer's hand at work, which will expose a lack of craft and potentially pull us out of the story.

A way to see if your characters are clearly distinguishable is to temporarily remove the character headings from your screenplay and then read the whole enchilada aloud. Ideally you should be able to figure out who's talking based on their distinctive speech patterns.

Foreign accents and syntax

As a general rule, if a foreign character speaks in English with an accent, their dialogue should be written using the grammar and syntax of their native tongue.

For example, let's say a character born in France is speaking English. A native English speaker would introduce themselves by saying, "My name is Claude." A native French speaker would introduce themselves in French by saying, "Je m'appelle Claude."

If translated directly into English, the character is actually saying, "I call myself Claude." So if you're writing a native French speaker who's using English, that's what they might say because—unless they're bilingual—they would likely default to French syntax.

As for their accent, don't write it into the dialogue by using words like "zis" or "zat" in place of "this" or "that," to use another French example. Using French syntax in English will suggest the accent, while both avoiding stereotypes and making it easier to read.

Dialects, idioms, colloquialisms, and slang

Other aspects of dialogue can also help to distinguish one character from another and they're usually associated with their origins. Where we're brought up invariably influences how we speak and how we choose to say what we say.

Dialects are ways of speaking that are common to specific regional or social groupings. Examples of differing regional dialects would be: Texas twang vs. Boston Brahmin or Oxford English vs. Scottish brogue. Examples of differing social dialects would be country club vs. urban ghetto or college academic vs. Joe Six-Pack.

Idioms are expressions whose meanings don't reflect the literal meaning of their words. A few examples of common idioms would include, "It's raining cats and dogs," or "I'm so hungry I could eat a cow" or "A penny for your thoughts."

Colloquialisms are words or phrases that are specific to certain regions. Texas has some gems like: "He's so low, he could walk under a snake's belly with his hat on" (i.e., he's not to be trusted) or "He's all hat and no cattle" (i.e., he's boastful). And the Australians have: "Chuck a sickie" (i.e., take a sick day) or "Spit the dummy" (i.e., throw a tantrum).

Slang words are informal, used in speech, and are typically used in a particular context or by a particular group of people. Revisiting Texans and Aussies, we have: "varmint" (Texan for "small animal") and "Tracky Dacks" (Australian for "sweat pants").

Common slang words like "ain't" are acceptable for use, as they're considered words. Online dictionaries can clarify if a piece of slang is a word or not. And there are specialized slang dictionaries including everything from jailhouse lingo to pirate speak.

Employing dialects, idioms, colloquialisms, and slang is much preferable to phonetically spelling out the dialect on the page, which is difficult to read. For example, it's okay to write dialogue such as, "I done seen a ghost" or "Let's don't do that," but it's not okay to write dialogue such as "I'm gittin' goin', so g'bye." And also try to avoid using non-words like "oughta," "woulda," "coulda," "shoulda" and the like.

Emphasis

Don't underline or CAPITALIZE dialogue in order to indicate emphasis. If you feel compelled to do so, what it might mean is that your sentences aren't clear enough on their own. Occasionally you might need to provide the desired emphasis by using one of these means, but try not to overuse them. Instead, see if the dialogue can be restructured so that the placement of the emphasis becomes more obvious.

Parentheticals

A **parenthetical** is a tool that can help clarify subtext. It's a qualifying word or words inserted in parentheses between the character heading and the dialogue. Parentheticals can indicate how a line should be read and/or indicate a concurrent action or activity.

Caution: don't overuse them. Some screenwriters (like me) have a tendency to try to direct their movie on the page, so we employ parentheticals to the point that the screenplay becomes tiresome to read and off-putting to the actors and director.

Here's an example of the correct use of a parenthetical:

> John smiles at Marsha and
> takes her by the hand.

> JOHN
> (smitten)
> You're something else.

Conversely, if a line reading should be the opposite of what's written, perhaps because the character is being sarcastic, you can also indicate it in the parenthetical.

> Marsha glares at John, seething.

> MARSHA
> (sarcastic)
> No, you're something else.

Truncating and overlapping

Other attributes of dialogue are 1) people rarely finish sentences, 2) people who know each other well often speak in half-sentences or use jargon and, 3) people sometimes speak at cross purposes on two different subjects simultaneously.

When two characters speak at the same time—talking over each other—your screenwriting software should have the capability to format dual columns of dialogue. You can also employ a parenthetical that says "**overlapping**," like so:

> JOHN   MARSHA
> (overlapping)   (overlapping)
> It's great to see you. I'm getting a divorce.

Keep it visual

Given that film is a visual medium, subtext can be communicated using body language or other onscreen clues. Dialogue should therefore be used judiciously, albeit with specific exceptions, as with a character who's a chatterbox. The rule of thumb is this: any dialogue where a character tells us something that we could have been shown should be rethought.

FILM EXAMPLES OF
SUBTEXT

CONTEMPORARY FILMS

Get Out

Activity: Having just met his daughter's boyfriend, Chris (Daniel Kaluuya), Dean Armitage (Bradley Whitford) tours him around his country mansion. Among other things, he shows Chris a photo of his father, a sprinter who was beat out for a spot on the Olympic team by Jessie Owens. Chris recalls that Owens won in Berlin and put the lie to Hitler's claim of Aryan superiority. Dean jokingly quips that his father almost got over it.

Subtext: While Dean is oozing white liberalism and tolerance, his comments here seem to suggest the opposite—that is, that there's an Armitage family history of resentment toward Black people.

The King's Speech

Activity: Under an assumed name, Elizabeth (Helena Bonham Carter) visits commoner Dr. Lionel Logue in his modest offices to talk to him about treating her husband—the Duke of York—for his stammer. As they converse, Logue realizes who she is, but doesn't show her any special deference.

Subtext: What Elizabeth isn't verbalizing is that she's desperate to alleviate her husband's unhappiness; that is, she's acting out of love. What Logue isn't verbalizing is that he won't be treated as a social inferior.

Moneyball

Activity: After their baseball team is eliminated from the playoffs, Peter Brand (Jonah Hill) shows downcast GM Billy Beane (Brad Pitt) a video in which a minor league hitter is humiliated when he wipes out rounding first base, until the hitter realizes he hit a home run. Peter is trying to show Billy that even though their baseball team didn't make it to the World Series, Billy still hit a home run. Billy smiles and tells Peter he's a "good egg," then exits.

Subtext: What Peter isn't verbalizing is "I'm your friend and I care about you," and in response, what Billy isn't verbalizing is "Thank you for being my friend."

The Phantom Thread

Activity: Early in the film, Reynolds (Daniel Day-Lewis) and his sister Cyril (Lesley Manville) are dining out, and Cyril offers to rid him of his current troublesome girlfriend, something it seems like she has done before and with some pleasure. Giving her his silent assent, he then laments about missing their dead mother.

Subtext: What we're learning is that Cyril is not only Reynolds's fixer, but she also thinks she's the only one who can effectively take care of her brother, whom we can see is a petulant man-child.

The Wolf of Wall Street

Activity: Newbie stockbroker Jordan Belfort (Leonardo DiCaprio) and jaded stockbroker veteran Mark Hanna (Matthew McConaughey) have lunch in a posh Wall Street restaurant. While snorting cocaine and imbibing serial martinis, Hanna gives Belfort outrageous advice on stockbroking and masturbation.

Subtext: What Hanna isn't verbalizing is that while he may be rich, he's also unhappy and lonely, which has made him a little crazy. What Belfort isn't verbalizing is that if this whacked-out guy can be a financial success, I too can be a financial success!

CLASSIC FILMS

Annie Hall

Activity: Annie (Diane Keaton) and Alvy (Woody Allen) are having an intellectual conversation about her photography and the nature of the artist's aesthetic.

Subtext: Annie and Alvy are attracted to each other but are both insecure. As a comic device, Woody Allen puts the subtext onscreen as subtitles, to hilarious effect.

Little Big Man

Activity: The Puritan Mrs. Pendrake (Faye Dunaway) imparts religious instruction to the "well-grown" Jack Crabb (Dustin Hoffman) as she gives him a much-needed bath.

Subtext: What the repressed Mrs. Pendrake isn't verbalizing is that she desperately wants to have mad hot sex with young, strapping Jack.

Ordinary People

Activity: Beth (Mary Tyler Moore) and her husband Calvin (Donald Sutherland) are having breakfast and engaging in small talk. Their fidgety son Conrad (Timothy Hutton) joins them. Beth puts French toast on Conrad's plate, but he says he's not hungry. She silently dumps the food down the garbage disposal and exits. Meanwhile, Calvin is overly pleased to hear that Conrad is getting together with his old school chums.

Subtext: Beneath the small talk, we see that Conrad suffers from anxiety due to some sort of trauma and that Calvin is very concerned about him; conversely, Beth is trying to suppress the resentment she harbors toward her son.

On the nose

Can you imagine the above scenes if the characters spoke the subtext aloud? It would make the audience cringe. When this occurs in a screenplay, the dialogue is called "**on the nose**," which means it is neither realistic nor true to life. Subtext: avoid such dialogue at all cost.

21

//

Minor Characters and Crowds

To name or not to name

Should **minor characters** have given names? If they're recurring characters, by all means. However, if they don't recur or they have little or no dialogue, then instead just provide them with generic names such as BARTENDER or FLIGHT ATTENDANT.

Their purpose in life and art

Minor characters are primarily used to serve a specific purpose, which is often to convey exposition. They can also be used to set up the genre, arena, tone, and ground rules. And they can offer commentary, stating what we're all thinking, often to comic effect.

Take the lady diner in *When Harry Met Sally* who, after hearing Sally convincingly fake an orgasm, turns to the waiter and, deadpan, says, "I'll have what she's having." This also demonstrates how one line of dialogue can be enough to fully define a minor character. *Every* character must be specific, no matter how small the part. They should have something that defines them so they aren't generic or one-dimensional.

Help define central characters

Minor characters usually can't exist independently without some relationship to the central characters. For instance, they can be used to help define the central characters by contrasting the central characters' abilities—or lack of abilities.

For example, at the beginning of *Phantom Thread*, Reynolds Woodcock has tired of his current dalliance Johanna to the point of hostility. She's sent away by Woodcock's sister Cyril, who's his fixer and first among equals.

When Woodcock next romances Alma, Cyril is confident she'll soon go the way of the others. But in contrast to Johanna, Alma displays a hidden strength that puts her in direct conflict with Cyril. In this case, minor characters Johanna and Cyril both help define Alma.

Give them action

If there's a minor character who does nothing but their job in a scene, always try to give them an action that will relate to the other characters. A common example is the nosy waitress who eavesdrops on a private conversation as she serves her customers. In addition to serving food and drink, she impinges on the characters' privacy.

Use in subplots

Minor characters can also be used in subplots to help illuminate the premise from other vantage points, which we'll
address in more detail in chapter 28.

〰〰〰〰〰〰〰〰〰〰〰〰〰〰〰〰〰〰〰〰〰〰〰〰〰〰〰〰〰〰〰〰〰〰〰〰〰〰〰

FILM EXAMPLES OF
MINOR CHARACTERS AND THEIR USES

CONTEMPORARY FILMS

The Blind Side

Scene: Leigh Anne (Sandra Bullock) has lunch with her socialite
friends.

Purpose: This is the second lunch date that Leigh Anne has with her
friends, and unlike the first lunch date, she's no longer able to
silently tolerate their patronizing tone and overt racism, so she
gives them a piece of her mind.

Minor characters: Beth, Elaine, and Sherry

Use: To help show the protagonist's character arc

Fences

Scene: It's late afternoon and Troy (Denzel Washington) is drinking
in a bar by himself when he's unexpectedly joined by his old
friend and former coworker Bono (Stephen Henderson).

Purpose: Bono, who once looked up to Troy, now won't have a drink
with him, signaling that Troy no longer has Bono's respect. After
more small talk, Bono departs to hang out with others, showing
that he has moved on, whereas Troy seems incapable of change.

Minor character: Bono

Use: To help show the protagonist's lack of growth

Roman J. Israel, Esq.

Scene: Maya (Carmen Ejogo) catches up with Roman (Denzel
Washington) as he's walking home after being heckled at a
speaking engagement. They encounter a homeless man lying
face down who they think is dead. The police arrive and become

aggressive. Roman slips his business card into the man's pocket so he won't be mass cremated. The police get more aggressive, but before they can arrest Roman, the homeless man revives and wanders away.

Purpose: Maya sees that Roman doesn't just talk the talk: he walks the walk. Out of compassion for his fellow man, he not only risks arrest, but will also assume the burial costs for a complete stranger. Maya is blown away.

Minor characters: Maya, the Homeless Man

Use: To help reveal the protagonist's character

We Need to Talk About Kevin

Scene: Town pariah Eva Khatchadourian (Tilda Swinton), the mother of a high school mass murderer, lands a job. She is elated as she leaves the job interview but then is sucker-punched by two angry women. A man tries to help her, but Eva takes all the blame and flees.

Purpose: In this gloomy character study, we're beginning to learn that Eva feels so guilty about how she raised her son that she perversely feels she "deserves" the wrath of the townsfolk and even more perversely believes that by enduring their cruelty, she can provide them with some catharsis for her son's evil deed.

Minor characters: Two female passers-by, a male stranger

Use: To help illustrate the protagonist's dominant character trait

Whiplash

Scene: At a diner, Andrew (Miles Teller) splits up with his girlfriend Nicole (Melissa Benoist), telling her that she'll just end up resenting him for putting his music career first and thus she'll be a hindrance to him becoming one of the greatest jazz drummers ever.

Purpose: This scene follows the family dinner scene and it shows that Andrew's blind ambition is changing him into someone callous and egotistical; that is, he's aping Terence Fletcher (J. K. Simmons), his sadistic teacher.

Minor character: Nicole

Use: To help show the protagonist's character arc

CLASSIC FILMS

The Mask

Scene: We meet Stanley Ipkiss (Jim Carrey) in the bank where he works. His coworker Maggie (Joely Fisher) bats her eyelashes and cons him out of concert tickets. His friend Charlie (Richard Jeni), who considers himself a ladies' man, tells Stanley that he's a doormat. Stanley says he's just a gentleman.

Purpose: The two minor characters help illustrate who Stanley is as a person. One uses him shamelessly and the other tells him he needs to be more assertive. So when Stanley finds the mask and discovers its powers, we understand why he thinks he needs to use it.

Minor characters: Maggie and Charlie

Use: To help illustrate the protagonist's dominant character trait

The Shawshank Redemption

Scene: Brooks (James Whitmore), the elderly librarian, is released from prison. He's not used to the pace of the modern world. He moves into a shabby rooming house and takes a job bagging groceries at a supermarket. One night, depressed, he carves his name into a wooden beam in his room, then hangs himself from it.

Purpose: Earlier in the film, while talking to Andy, Red (Morgan Freeman) explains how being an "institutionalized man" means that once you've been in prison for many years, you can no longer handle freedom. Brooks is an example of this phenomenon. When Red is paroled and moves into the same rooming house, we worry that this may also be his fate.

Minor character: Brooks

Use: To provide contrast to the protagonist

Tootsie

Scene: Unemployed actor Michael Dorsey (Dustin Hoffman)—posing as Dorothy Michaels—is having her first screen test. The producer, Rita Marshall (Doris Belack), says she would like to make Dorothy more attractive and asks the cameraman how far he can pull back, to which he replies, "How do you feel about Cleveland?"

Purpose: This scene addresses whether it's plausible that people won't spot that Dorothy is a man. By having a minor character say that she's not very attractive (and do it with humor), it allows us to suspend our disbelief. We no longer question whether the ruse will be successful.

Minor characters: Rita Marshall, Cameraman

Use: To provide comic relief by saying aloud what everyone else is thinking

Use of Crowds

It's been said that mobs have a personality. In film, crowds, similar to minor characters, can help to define the world around them and illuminate or provide contrast to the central characters in a story.

Defining society

How crowds treat an event will help define the society they live in and its morality. For example, you might remember the scene in *Midnight Cowboy* where New Yorkers walk blithely past an unconscious man who is lying face down on the sidewalk.

Crowd character

Crowds should have a specifically described character, like an individual. In other words, a crowd is a conglomerate character with an attitude and a point of view. One or two people in a crowd can define how the entire crowd feels by their words or deeds.

Help define central characters

Akin to individual minor characters, a crowd can help reveal a protagonist through contrast or by acting on the protagonist in some way. In *Midnight Cowboy*, Joe Buck's innocence is revealed by his reaction to the passers-by ignoring the prostrate man on the sidewalk.

Budgetary consideration

Unless you don't have to worry about budget, try to avoid including a crowd unless it's organic and has a defined purpose that can't be achieved another, less expensive way.

FILM EXAMPLES OF
CROWD SCENES

CONTEMPORARY FILMS

About a Boy

Scene: To show that he loves his mother, young Marcus (Nicholas Hoult) is about to commit social suicide by singing "Killing me Softly" a cappella at his high school talent show, when Will Freeman (Hugh Grant) walks onstage and accompanies him on the guitar to distract the malevolent teen audience.

Crowd attitude: Ridicule

I, Robot

Scene: Spooner (Will Smith) and Calvin (Bridget Moynahan), looking for the rogue robot that will come to be known as Sonny, enter the factory floor at US Robotics where 101 identical robots await. Spooner finally tricks Sonny into revealing himself and the rogue robot tries to escape.

Crowd attitude: Camouflage

I, Tonya

Scene: Early in the film, Tonya (Margot Robbie) skates brilliantly and the crowd roars with approval. However, by the time she performs at the Olympics in Lillehammer, she's jeered by the crowd. After she's banned from skating and takes up boxing, the crowd is even more hateful, cheering when she's knocked out.

Crowd attitude: Approbation, then scorn, then hatred

The King's Speech

Scene: In the opening scene of the film, Bertie (Colin Firth) is to deliver a speech live in a stadium and on radio and he's terrified due to his stammer. As he struggles to speak, we see the reaction of the assembled crowd.

Crowd attitude: Embarrassment

V for Vendetta

Scene: Citizens take to the streets in Guy Fawkes masks and confront the military who, outnumbered, stand down.

Crowd attitude: Revolution

CLASSIC FILMS

Dave

Scene: Dave (Kevin Kline) is hired to impersonate the president for security reasons. When he emerges from a hotel and heads to a limo, the waiting crowd bursts into applause. Nervous at first, he slowly gets into it and starts to wave back, then yells, "God Bless America" to the crowd, before the secret service stuffs him into the limo.

Crowd attitude: Approbation

Invasion of the Body Snatchers

Scene: People are walking around expressionless and without affect because they've been turned into pod people, and if they see a human showing emotion, they'll shriek and alert the authorities.

Crowd attitude: Threat

The Last Emperor

Scene: When the newly crowned child emperor (Richard Vuu) is presented at court in the Forbidden City, he walks outside where thousands of monks chant and genuflect to him.

Crowd attitude: Adulation

22

\\

Flashbacks and Flash-Forwards

A **flashback** is a scene or sequence that jumps back in time and a **flash-forward** is a scene or sequence that jumps forward in time. I was taught to avoid using flashbacks, as they were considered a cheat because they were primarily used to deliver exposition.

My thoughts on this topic have evolved. I think it's fine to use either a flashback or flash-forward if it's motivated organically. Here's some scenarios where flashbacks and flash-forwards would be considered organic:

- an amnesiac trying to recall their identity;
- a mentally ill person having delusions;
- a war veteran suffering from Post-Traumatic Stress Disorder;
- a psychic having some kind of vision;
- a Walter Mitty–type character who daydreams;

- a drug user experiencing hallucinations; or
- a traumatic memory that resurfaces.

An example of an inorganic flashback would be a story that takes place in the present, except for one scene where we flash back to see a protagonist's relationship with a family member when they were a child, which is meant to explain some present-day conflict. Since the flashback isn't organically motivated and is stylistically inconsistent with the rest of the story, it stands out as blatant exposition. Audiences would eat it for lunch.

FILM EXAMPLES OF
FLASHBACKS AND FLASH-FORWARDS

CONTEMPORARY FILMS

Dallas Buyers Club

Scene: Ron Woodroof (Matthew McConaughey) scoffs at his HIV diagnosis but then goes to the library to research the disease. When he sees the words "intravenous drug use" on the microfiche, he remembers having unprotected sex with a woman who had a snake tattoo...and needle marks on her arm.

Device: Flashback

I Am Legend

Scene: In post-apocalyptic New York, Robert Neville (Will Smith) is the last man left alive due to a genetically modified virus. We go back and forth and see his relationship with his wife, son, and dog and see how New York slowly became a wasteland.

Device: Flashback

I, Robot

Scene: Spooner (Will Smith) has been having intermittent nightmares involving a crash and fire and we see that he was involved in a car wreck where he was saved by a robot, but in the process, he lost his arm, which helps explain why he hates robots.

Device: Flashback

Lion

Scene: Saroo (Dev Patel) has random memories of his childhood that serve as a memory map to help him try to locate the village in India where he was born and where his birth family resides.

Device: Flashback

Minority Report

Scene: In the opening scene of the film, which is the first of many such sequences, images of a murder that has yet to be committed are visualized by "pre-cogs."

Device: Flash-forward

Sherlock Holmes

Scene: Sherlock (Robert Downey Jr.) is in a bare-knuckle fight with a big palooka. He tries to concede the fight, but to no avail. He then pre-visualizes the rest of the fight in slow motion, narrating his planned strategy.

Device: Flash-forward

CLASSIC FILMS

Ordinary People

Scene: Conrad Jarrett (Timothy Hutton) has a panic attack when he learns that his friend Karen (Dinah Manoff) has committed suicide. He races to his psychiatrist, Dr. Berger (Judd Hirsch), who helps him relive a boating accident in which his older brother drowned.

Device: Flashback

Terminator

Scene: As Reese (Michael Biehn) tells Sarah Connor (Linda Hamilton) why he's traveled through time to save her life, we get a glimpse of the dystopian future.

Device: Flash-forward

23

\\

Montage and Series of Shots

Montage and **series of shots** are two techniques used to bridge time. Rather than employing individual scenes, a series of shots or montage compress the action into a condensed sequence in order to move quickly through a section of the story.

Beginning, middle, and end

Both techniques have a beginning, middle, and end. Each shot incrementally advances the sequence in the same way that every scene incrementally advances a narrative. And similar to the beginning and ending of a story, things have changed in some tangible way by the end of a montage or a series of shots, often some kind of advancement.

No dialogue

Both techniques are usually played against music and/or sound effects with little or no dialogue. Whether there's dialogue or not, these sequences are primarily visual. The visuals may contain either realistic or fantastic imagery or a mix of both.

The difference between series of shots and montage

A series of shots is sequential—each shot chronologically follows the next shot, while a montage can be out of chronological sequence and can have multiple images onscreen simultaneously via superimpositions, slow dissolves, or split screens.

In addition, a series of shots almost always features the central characters, while a montage is more abstract and thus may or may not feature the central characters. For instance, a dream sequence or a hallucinogenic sequence may not show the central character but rather would show their visual stream of consciousness from their point of view.

Series of shots

A classic series of shots is the "falling in love" sequence, where at the beginning, a couple is just starting their romance and by the end, they've fallen in love. The sequence abridges the lengthy time span of a courtship so that the story can maintain pace.

Another example is a "traveling" sequence, where a character or characters are traveling from point A to point B. Here again, there has to be a change from how they are at the beginning of the journey to the end of the journey. For example, on a wartime forced march, the prisoners start out healthy but by the end, they're at death's door.

Montage

Montages are often used to bridge or compress time but can also have other uses. Because the images can be superimposed and/or visually altered, a montage can contain dreams, nightmares, drug experiences, hallucinations, combat flashbacks, and more.

Rhythm

A story should be dynamic. It should have highs and lows and it should vary in pace. A montage or series of shots, whether frenetic or leisurely in pace, is a sequence that breaks up the ongoing scene-by-scene narrative. If you feel the narrative is dragging at a certain point and you can use one of these techniques to help compress time, then that's a good reason to employ them.

FILM EXAMPLES OF
SERIES OF SHOTS AND MONTAGES

CONTEMPORARY FILMS

I, Tonya

Sequence: After placing fourth at the Olympics in Albertville, France, Tonya (Margo Robbie) goes back to waitressing, but her coach, Diane (Julianne Nicholson), convinces her to give it another try. Tonya relents and goes into a training sequence that also includes her developing a more "all-American" image.

Technique: Series of shots

Marie Antoinette

Sequence: To show Marie Antoinette's penchant for overindulgence, this sequence shows Marie (Kirsten Dunst) and her friends eating French pastries, trying on fancy shoes, and having their hair done, all set to a cover of the song "I Want Candy" by Bow Wow Wow.

Technique: Montage

Moneyball

Sequence: Using Peter Brand's system, the Oakland A's go on a record-setting twenty-game winning streak. The sequence blends stock footage from the actual games/broadcasts with filmed footage. The sequence is actually introduced by a title card that reads, "The Streak."

Technique: Series of shots

Team America: World Police

Sequence: A sequence in the film is in fact a parody of a montage and is set to a gag song called "Montage." Sample lyrics: "Show a lot of things happening at once / Remind everyone of what's going on (what's going on?) / And with every shot you show a little improvement / To show it all would take too long / That's called a montage."

Technique: Montage

The Wolf of Wall Street

Sequence: After moving his brokerage from an old auto garage to a proper office space, Jordan Belfort (Leonardo DiCaprio) sets his seventy-five brokers loose on the phone. In a rapid sequence spanning several months, we cut back and forth as they unleash their sales pitches on the phone to clients. The business is exploding, which is confirmed in the next scene, when Jordan reports the sales figures.

Technique: Series of shots

CLASSIC FILMS

Apocalypse Now

Sequence: Set to "The End" by the Doors, in the opening scene of the film, Captain Willard (Martin Sheen) is drinking in a Saigon hotel room waiting for his next assignment. As he looks up at the ceiling fan, it juxtaposes with helicopter rotor blades and memories of a jungle napalm attack. This results in a psychotic episode, exposing his fragile state of mind.

Technique: Montage

Ghostbusters

Sequence: After successfully finishing their first job, the Ghostbusters are suddenly everywhere: newspapers, TV, magazines, and radio. Success has a price, however, as they're worked to the point of exhaustion. Set to the tune "Ghostbusters," performed by Ray Parker Jr.

Technique: Montage

Pretty Woman

Sequence: Edward (Richard Gere) sends Vivian (Julia Roberts) out shopping for upscale fashions with his credit card and instructions to spend an obscene amount of money. We see her transform from "trash to class," set to the song "Pretty Woman," performed by Roy Orbison.

Technique: Series of shots

Scarface

Sequence: We see Tony Montana (Al Pacino) achieving the American Dream by drug trafficking and killing. He expands into legitimate business and marries a trophy wife who has a cocaine habit. Set to the disco song "Push It to the Limit," performed by Paul Engemann.

Technique: Series of shots

Toy Story 2

Sequence: One of the most emotional moments in the film is the sequence where Jesse (Joan Cusack) remembers when Emily played with her as a child, but then as Emily grew up she lost interest in toys, finally donating Jesse to charity. Set to the Sarah McLachlan tune "When She Loved Me."

Technique: Series of shots

24

////////////////////////////////////

Time Transitions

Sometimes stuck writers paint themselves into a corner by having two scenes back to back in the same location with a time transition in between, where a night has passed or a season has passed or several years have passed. They need some kind of **time transition**, which is a visual technique to show the passage of time.

It can be problematic to dissolve from one location to the very same location, leaving the audience unclear on how *much* time has elapsed between the two scenes. The solution is to select a detail that's organic to the location to indicate the passage of time, such as one of the following:

- a candle that's burned down;
- hands or numbers on a clock that have advanced;
- ice in a glass (or an ice sculpture) that has melted;
- a filling bathtub that's now overflowing;
- day turns into night or vice versa; or
- a change of season(s).

Time transitions can be extremely creative and novel.

FILM EXAMPLES OF
TIME TRANSITIONS

CONTEMPORARY FILMS

A Beautiful Mind

Sequence: John Nash (Russell Crowe) gets an inspiration in the
bar and goes back to his dormitory room to work on a new
mathematical proof. As we pull back from his window, it slowly
stops snowing and the trees grow foliage.

Time transition: Winter passes

Gangs of New York

Sequence: In a series of dissolves showing the city of New York
evolving into the modern era, the graveyard of the gang
members becomes overgrown until it's finally gone, along with
the memories of those who sacrificed their lives.

Time transition: 1846 to 2002

Slumdog Millionaire

Sequence: Two brothers, nine-year-old Salim (Azharuddin
Mohammed Ismail) and seven-year-old Jamal (Ayush Mahesh
Khedekar), get caught stealing food on a train and they jump off.
They tumble head over heels into a ditch, and when they sit up,
they're teenagers, age fourteen and twelve.

Time transition: Five years pass

The Time Machine

Sequence: When Wells (Rod Taylor) tests the machine and moves
forward into the future, flowers grow and die, clocks speed up,
buildings are erected, and technology advances. An interesting
detail is that the style of the clothes on a mannequin in a store
window across the street rapidly changes.

Time transition: Hundreds of years pass

Zodiac

Sequence: As the reporters and police chase down clues, we see

San Francisco's iconic Transamerica skyscraper being built in a time-lapse sequence.

Time transition: A year passes

CLASSIC FILMS

Close Encounters of the Third Kind

Sequence: Roy (Richard Dreyfuss) falls asleep at the dining room table and is awakened the next morning by the sound of goofy TV cartoons. Notably, the time transition is achieved with lighting and sound; that is, it's all the same shot.

Time transition: Night turns into day

Notting Hill

Sequence: After being dumped by Anna (Julia Roberts) when hordes of paparazzi find them together at his apartment, a depressed Will (Hugh Grant) takes a stroll down Portobello Road as the seasons change around him.

Time transition: A year passes

Counteraction

Counteraction can be described as something that's happening in a scene that either comments on or contrasts with the action, yielding irony. A common example is a life-or-death foot chase that happens among a holiday street parade. The revelry of the parade serves as counteraction to the intense and potentially lethal foot chase.

While irony is delicious for a writer, the principal function of counteraction is to provide an obstacle, which helps ramp up the conflict. In the chase example above, if there were no parade, the pursuers would more easily be able to track and capture their quarry.

Organic

Counteraction can't just appear out of nowhere. It has to be organic to the arena, the locale, the time of year, and so forth. There should be setups earlier in the narrative where, again using the above example, we learn that it's St. Patrick's Day or Chinese New Year. The payoff is the festive parade that later intersects and impedes the chase sequence.

Location

A location can be enough to counter the action of a scene. For example, a married couple can have an argument at a stand-up comedy club. While they're in the audience angrily hissing at each other, everyone around them is laughing at the comic onstage.

A movie example can be found in Woody Allen's *Manhattan* in the scene set in a planetarium. The self-involved characters are complaining about their personal problems as they walk among images of the cosmos, making their issues seem petty in comparison.

Covering dialogue

Counteraction doesn't advance the story, but it can cover dialogue that advances the story, especially if the characters are static. A great example can be found in the movie *When Harry Met Sally* in the scene where Harry and his friend attend a baseball game. Depressed, Harry bitterly recounts details of his recent divorce, while every ten seconds they have to stand up and cheer when a "wave" circles around the stadium.

〜〜〜〜〜〜〜〜〜〜〜〜〜〜〜〜〜〜〜〜〜〜〜〜〜〜〜〜〜〜〜〜〜〜

FILM EXAMPLES OF
COUNTERACTION

CONTEMPORARY FILMS

The Big Short

Scene: Mark Baum (Steve Carell) is meeting with a topless stripper in a VIP room, having paid for her time. He's trying to understand her real estate practices and the local mortgage market while she continues to bump and grind.

Counteraction function: Contrast

Her

Scene: Theodore (Joaquin Phoenix) is seated on the subways steps talking to Samantha (Scarlett Johansson). People pass by, happily talking with their own operating systems. Samantha admits she multitasks when she's conversing with Theodore. Concerned, he asks if she's in love with anyone else and, if so, how many. She says 641, which really upsets him. His upset contrasts with the happiness of the people passing by him.

Counteraction function: Contrast

Mission Impossible: Rogue Nation

Scene: At the Vienna Opera House during a packed performance of *Turandot,* Ethan Hunt (Tom Cruise) leaps into action high up in the fly rigging to stop snipers from assassinating the Austrian chancellor without causing a panic in the audience.

Counteraction function: Obstacle

Spectre

Scene: After killing some would-be assassins, James Bond (Daniel Craig) chases assassin Marco Sciarra (Alessandro Cremona) through the Day of the Dead parade in Mexico City.

Counteraction function: Obstacle

CLASSIC FILMS

The Fugitive

Scene: Dr. Richard Kimble (Harrison Ford), surreptitiously doing research at a hospital, is spotted by US Marshall Samuel Gerard (Tommy Lee Jones). Kimble races out into the street, where the St. Patrick's Day parade is underway. The two men play cat and mouse until Kimble manages to melt away into the crowd.

Counteraction function: Obstacle

The Godfather

Scene: Michael (Al Pacino) and Kay (Diane Keaton) attend the baptism of Connie's baby. While the priest chants the rite and the pipe organ swells, we cross-cut to Michael's henchmen, who are on a killing spree at his behest.

Counteraction function: Contrast

Heathers

Scene: At Heather Chandler's (Kim Walker) solemn funeral, as her friends pray solemnly beside her open casket, we can hear their thoughts, which reveal they're all massively self-involved.

Counteraction function: Contrast

26

Time Locks

A **time lock** is a deadline. The most obvious example is a
ticking bomb. However, it doesn't always have to be clock-ori-
ented. It could be the impending birth of a child. Or it could be
the date of a building demolition. Or it could be the hour of an
execution.

Finiteness gives form

Time locks are used to exert pressure on the story, especially
in Act III. The writer and the audience know exactly when the
climax and resolution must occur: just before—or simultaneously—with the expiration of the time lock.

Not for every film

While time locks are useful, not all films have time locks, nor
do they need them. In *Good Will Hunting*, we have no idea
that Will is going to make a breakthrough with therapist Sean
Maguire until it happens. Psychotherapy is a process that defies
end dates.

~~~~~~

FILM EXAMPLES OF

TIME LOCKS

CONTEMPORARY FILMS

The Hurt Locker

Scene: An innocent Iraqi civilian approaches a US bomb unit, begging them to help remove the suicide vest he's wearing, which is set to detonate in two minutes. Unfortunately, they can't remove it in time and it explodes.

Time lock: Bomb timer

The Martian

Scene: While there are many things that can go wrong that will end his life, astronaut Mark Watney (Matt Damon) is constantly calculating how many sols—Martian days—he has remaining before his supplies expire or when the *Ares* crew will return to rescue him.

Time lock: Finite supplies

Mission Impossible: Ghost Protocol

Scene: A nuclear missile is launched from a submarine toward San Francisco and Ethan Hunt (Tom Cruise) has just three minutes to disable it.

Time lock: Missile detonation

Room

Scene: Ma (Alison Brie) is told by Old Nick (Sean Bridgers) that he's been laid off from his job and money is now tight. She realizes that if Old Nick doesn't get a job soon, she and Jack (Jacob Tremblay) may be left to die of starvation. Escape becomes imperative.

Time lock: Possibility of starvation

Still Alice

Scene: Alice (Julianne Moore), diagnosed with Alzheimer's disease, makes a video for herself with a set of questions that, when she's unable to answer them, means it's time for her to commit suicide with pills.

Time lock: Dementia

CLASSIC FILMS

Alien

Scene: The computer executes a countdown to the moment where the ship *Nostromo* and everything aboard it will be destroyed.

Time lock: Auto-destruct mechanism

DOA

Scene: *Professor Dexter Cornell (Dennis Quaid) has thirty-six hours to find out who poisoned him, before the poison takes effect and he dies.*

Time lock: *Lethal poison*

High Noon

Scene: Noon is the appointed hour when the vengeful Miller Gang is going to arrive in Hadleyville to kill Marshal Will Kane (Gary Cooper).

Time lock: Noon

27

Props and Telephones

A **prop**—which is something that a character can hold in their hand (or hands)—shouldn't be *specifically* described unless it's important either to the plot or to the illustration of character. Once a prop is particularized, it becomes a setup that must be paid off later. If not, it becomes a red herring which, as we know, is undesirable.

However, if a prop *is* particularized, it should have specificity in order to help reveal character and/or other information. Ask yourself what specific physical objects your character would choose. There's obviously a difference between someone who carries a Swiss army knife and a someone who packs a switchblade.

FILM EXAMPLES OF
PARTICULARIZED PROPS

CONTEMPORARY FILMS

Cast Away

Prop: A volleyball

Particularization: Marooned on a tropical island, Chuck Noland helps alleviate his loneliness by befriending a volleyball. Once he paints on a face, the volleyball seems more human and he calls it Wilson, which is also its brand name.

The King's Speech

Prop: The BBC microphone

Particularization: Every time Bertie faces this rather intimidating prop, it sends him into a state of panic. This is partly because of its size and partly because it represents his subjects, the British public, who are out there glued to their radios.

No Country for Old Men

Prop: A captive bolt pistol

Particularization: Normally used to stun cattle, having Anton Chigurh (Javier Bardem) use this device to kill people provides three benefits: 1) victims don't know it's lethal until it's too late; 2) it shows that Chigurh is a sadistic psychopath; and 3) the thing is terrifying.

The Ring

Prop: A VHS videocassette

Particularization: Whenever anyone watches this VHS video, they die within seven days. The fact that this prop is such a common household object made it even scarier. Everyone owns VHS cassettes, right?

Whiplash

Prop: Bloody drumsticks

Particularization: After being humiliated by Fletcher (J. K. Simmons), Andrew Neiman (Miles Teller) practices drumming so intensely that his hands begin to bleed. The bloody drumsticks show not only his resolve to prove Fletcher wrong, but also his desire to be one of the greatest drummers ever.

CLASSIC FILMS

Close Encounters of the Third Kind

Prop: Mashed potatoes

Particularization: At the dinner table, Roy Neary (Richard Dreyfuss) tries to sculpt the form of a mysterious object that he can't stop visualizing using mashed potatoes. He's so obsessed, it causes his family to worry that he is losing his mind.

Harold and Maude

Prop: The Odorifics machine

Particularization: Maude shows Harold a device that can store and release bottled odors to provide sense memories. It's such a unique item, it helps to show both her sense of wonder and her tactile sensuality.

The Maltese Falcon

Prop: A jewel-encrusted statuette of a falcon

Particularization: Probably one of the most famous props in film history, this statuette and other such props were described by Alfred Hitchcock as "MacGuffins," which are ostensibly valuable objects that help drive the plot forward, but turn out to be unimportant.

Phone calls

Props such as telephones are singled out for some extra scrutiny in this chapter because they're so ubiquitous in movies. Let's first take a moment to define "**phone call**," because real-time communications have expanded way beyond telephones.

There's also telegraphs, intercoms, walkie-talkies, ham radios and CB radios. And in our modern era we would also include mobile phones, smart watches, VOIP calls, texting, and doubtless other high-tech devices that have yet to be invented.

Who's onscreen?

When considering the use of this specialized prop, here's a primary consideration: what side of a phone call should we see? Here are the choices:

1. Just see the caller
2. Intercut between both callers
3. Use a split screen and see both callers simultaneously
4. Superimpose text, which is happening a lot now with the advent of text messaging, where we see onscreen dialogue balloons containing the messages

Sometimes seeing the *reaction* to what's being said is more important than seeing it spoken by the person who's saying it.

Or sometimes it's desirable to only show one side of the conversation, like when one of the callers shouldn't be identified, such as an anonymous caller.

Other times it's important to see them both at the same time so we can simultaneously witness their reactions or perhaps the reactions of someone in the room with them.

To avoid confusing the audience, it's customary not to mix techniques, but it does happen. I've seen phone calls where the first half of the call we're on the caller and the last half of the call we're on the person on the other end of the line.

At the end of the day, the choice of how to handle telephone calls should be dictated by what's right for the story. Defying convention for the sake of said defiance can be an expression of artistic independence, but self-defeating if it's the wrong choice.

Writing one-sided conversations

Last thing. If for story reasons it's important to hear only one side of the phone conversation, first write both sides of the conversation, then delete the side we don't hear to ensure that we can still infer what's being said by the offscreen party.

FILM EXAMPLES OF
PHONE CALLS

CONTEMPORARY FILMS

Frequency

Scene: Massive solar storms disrupt radio communications and enable New York City policeman John Sullivan (Jim Caviezel) to speak over a ham (shortwave) radio to his father, Frank Sullivan (Dennis Quaid), a firefighter who died thirty years earlier.

Device/Type: Ham radio/two-sided—this communication device was chosen because ham radios exist in both time periods.

Mean Girls

Scene: The "Plastics" have a four-way phone conversation.

Device/Type: Home phones/split-screen—showing the girls onscreen all at the same time emphasizes the "conspiratorial" nature of their communications.

Ocean's Eleven

Scene: A mobile phone rings in Tess's (Julia Roberts) coat pocket. Benedict (Andy Garcia) tells her to answer it. She says she doesn't have a cell phone. He answers it and what follows is a long phone conversation between Rusty (Brad Pitt) and Benedict in which Benedict is told that he is being robbed and that he must comply with instructions or he will lose $160 million dollars. Benedict feigns compliance and advises Rusty to "run and hide."

Device/Type: Cell phone/two-sided—we see that Rusty is calling from the casino floor because he purposely wants the call to be traced to his location so that Benedict will know that he's in the casino.

Phone Booth

Scene: Stu Shephard (Colin Farrell) is trapped inside a phone booth by a mysterious caller who wants him to atone for his philandering.

Device/Type: Pay phone/one-sided—the concept is that we can't identify the caller—other than by his voice—until the end of the film.

CLASSIC FILMS

Airplane

Scene: The "Roger Roger" scene where the pilots talk to the airport tower and their cross-talk is like an Abbot and Costello routine.

Device/Type: Radio/one-sided—in this film nothing is sacred, including sending up how airline pilots communicate with controllers.

All the President's Men

Scene: Reporter Bob Woodward (Robert Redford) juggles lines as he tracks down the Watergate money trail on the phone.

Device/Type: Office phone/one-sided—by necessity, there were a lot of phone calls in this script, so they decided to film them in real time. This meant that rather than adding the offscreen voice in post-production, there were actual actors on the other end of the phone line as they filmed, which added authenticity.

The Matrix

Scene: Phones are the way into and out of the Matrix. The last call is from Neo (Keanu Reeves) to the machines.

Device/Type: Pay phone/one-sided—since phones are common objects, they're the "escape hatches" from the Matrix.

Notting Hill

Scene: Will Thacker (Hugh Grant) goes to visit Anna (Julia Roberts) on a movie set. He's handed a headset by the sound recordist and can hear her chatting with an actor between takes. Unaware that her microphone is on, when asked about Will, she shrugs and says he's "no one."

Device/Type: Headset/one-sided—an open microphone is used to create a misunderstanding, and as there's no opportunity for Will to reply, he departs, dejected.

28

Subplots

Subplots typically involve supporting characters and may or may not involve the protagonist. Depending on the length of a screenplay, there can be multiple subplots. Obviously, the shorter the screenplay, the less screen time there is for subplots. In some cases there are no subplots, for instance in stories that contain just a few characters.

Subplots can have their own climax and resolution prior to the main climax, or they can resolve at the same time as the main climax. Occasionally, they can resolve following the main climax, that is, during the resolution as the dust settles.

For example, in the film *About a Boy*, the story resolves with Will hanging out at home with his new family and concluding that "Every man is an island. And I stand by that. But clearly, some men are part of island chains" (which is a pay-off, by the way). So lessons have been learned, the characters have grown, and the dust is settling nicely.

However, there's some unfinished business. Marcus's single mom Fiona has been battling depression. She's prepping food in the kitchen where we see that Will has invited an old coworker. Clearly the two of them are cut from the same ex-hippie cloth, and so there's the hint of some sort of happiness for Fiona, which ties up this subplot.

In series television, a subplot may simply be a "B" story line. For example, in a detective procedural, there may be an "A" plot, which is the primary case that needs to be solved, and there may be "B" and "C" plots, which are secondary/tertiary cases and/or personal story lines that primarily involve the supporting characters.

In movies, ideally a subplot should illuminate the premise of the story, albeit from another direction. In fact, a subplot could prove the *corollary* of the premise and in so doing, serve to further reinforce the validity of the premise. I'll explain.

Let's take a story with the premise "courage gains freedom." The protagonist's dominant character trait is courage, and by being brave, the protagonist gains freedom. The writer is simply saying that in order to gain freedom, courage is required.

In this same story, there may be a subplot in which a supporting character commits a cowardly act, perhaps one of betrayal. The consequence of this act is incarceration. So the premise of this subplot might be "cowardice warrants punishment." The writer has to believe both statements are true and that both align with their point of view.

Whether a subplot is meant to illuminate the premise from another direction or is simply a second or third story line that interweaves with the main story line, the thing they all have in common is that they each must have their own beginning, middle, and end.

FILM EXAMPLES OF
SUBPLOTS

CONTEMPORARY FILMS

Erin Brockovich

Logline: Single mom Erin Brockovich (Julia Roberts) uncovers evidence that hundreds of people are battling serious health problems due to leaking hexavalent chromium from a PG&E plant. She spearheads a class-action lawsuit and PG&E is ordered by the court to pay a $333 million settlement.

Subplot and function: Erin enters into a romantic relationship with George (Aaron Eckhart), a biker, who helps take care of her kids. But her focus on her work leaves him feeling like a lesser priority, so they split up. The subplot shows the personal sacrifices that Erin makes for her quest.

Flight

Logline: Airline pilot and alcoholic Whip Whitaker (Denzel Washington) makes an extraordinary landing when his jet malfunctions. At an NTSB hearing, tired of lying, he admits that he's an alcoholic. Sent to prison, he's finally sober and grateful for his recovery.

Subplot and function: Nicole Maggen (Kelly Reilly) is a heroin addict who overdoses and meets Whittaker in the hospital. They begin a relationship, but she's trying to get clean, and Whittaker is still in denial. For her own well-being she decides to leave him. Her story contrasts with his because she acknowledges she has a problem, but he isn't yet ready to do so.

Hidden Figures

Logline: In the 1960s, Dorothy Vaughan (Octavia Spencer), Mary Jackson (Janelle Monáe), and Katherine Johnson (Taraji P. Henson) work at NASA at the height of the space race and have to battle overt racism and sexism in order to be recognized and valued.

Subplot and function: All three women battle intolerance, yet each also has her own story line. Dorothy wants to be promoted to supervisor, a job she's already doing. Katherine wants to be treated as an equal to the male employees, and Mary wants to go to college and earn an engineering degree. Each of their personal stories illuminates different aspects of the historical struggle for racial and gender equality in America.

The King's Speech

Logline: King George VI (Colin Firth) has a terrible stammer, and he finally agrees to undergo treatment with speech therapist Lionel Logue (Geoffrey Rush). The two men butt heads but eventually become friends. George must address his country via radio at the onset of World War II. With Logue's help, he nails the speech, showing he has the mettle to be a leader.

Subplot and function: Bertie's brother Edward, who's the heir to the throne, is in a romantic relationship with an American divorcee, Wallace Simpson. Wanting to marry her, he opts to abdicate, which forces Bertie to become king. This subplot depicts Edward as weak and selfish, which contrasts with his brother Bertie, who will make a better king.

Million Dollar Arm

Logline: J. B. Bernstein (Jon Hamm) is a baseball agent who gets the idea of bringing some Indian cricket players to the United States for MLB tryouts as pitchers. At first it's something of a publicity stunt that J. B. hopes to convert to cash, but then he begins to know his young charges and decides their welfare is more important than his avaricious schemes.

Subplot and function: J. B.'s tenant Brenda (Lake Bell), a nurse, learns what he's doing and is supportive. The two get romantically involved, but when Brenda sees J. B. is just using the boys, she gives him a piece of her mind. When J. B. later stops being selfish and starts to show them compassion, he and Brenda get back on track romantically.

CLASSIC FILMS

Awakenings

Logline: In 1969, Dr. Malcolm Sayer (Robin Williams) discovers that the drug L-Dopa can "awaken" patients that suffer from a form of sleeping sickness. Tragically, however, the drug proves to be only a temporary cure, and after several months of awareness, the patients go back to sleep.

Subplot and function: Patient Leonard Lowe (Robert De Niro) develops a romantic relationship with Paula (Penelope Ann Miller), the daughter of another patient. However, when Leonard realizes that he's regressing, in a heart-wrenching scene, he tells Paula that he can't see her anymore. His courage and loss inspires Dr. Sayer to get up the nerve to ask his head nurse out for coffee.

Notting Hill

Logline: Charming but cautious London bookstore owner Will Thacker (Hugh Grant) meets lonely American movie star Anna Scott (Julia Roberts). The two fall in love, but her celebrity status and his fear of being hurt emotionally keep getting in the way, until he takes a risk at a press conference by publically professing his love for her and she reciprocates.

Subplot and function: There are two romantic subplots. One is the relationship between Will's friends Max (Tom McInnerny) and Bella (Gina McKee). Their loving bond represents what William wants in a relationship. The other is the evolving romance between Will's slovenly roommate Spike (Rhys Ifans) and his Bohemian sister, Honey (Emma Chambers). Their romance shows that there is someone for everyone.

Parenthood

Logline: In this ensemble film, Gil Buckman (Steve Martin) and his extended family deal with the joys and challenges of being parents.

Subplot and function: After many years away, Larry Buckman (Tom Hulce), the family black sheep, arrives home with a young son named "Cool" and in need of money to pay off loan sharks. Gil pays off his irresponsible son's debts and agrees to take care of Cool while Larry leaves to chase another pipe dream. This subplot is meant to show that we never stop being parents at any age.

Twists

Spoiler alert: This chapter is going to ruin the films below for you if you haven't yet seen them. You've been warned!

Logic

Twists are sudden and unexpected plot turns that surprise the audience. Although twists are unexpected, they must be logical, which demands a lot of subtle setups. If a twist comes out of nowhere or isn't logical, it will fail the Parking Lot Test miserably. "Logical" in this context means that when we retro-actively evaluate the twist, it makes complete sense, based on the established facts of the story.

Timing

A twist can happen anywhere in the story. In *The Crying Game*, there are three identifiable twists. At the end of Act I, the incident that spins the story in another direction is when Jody escapes from his IRA captors, only to be run over and

killed by an armored carrier. We weren't expecting his character to be so prematurely eliminated.

Fergus, Jody's reluctant captor, then goes to London and
seeks out Jody's girlfriend, Dil, and the two of them grow close.
She's very mysterious and Fergus soon finds out exactly why
in a love scene, when he discovers that Dil is male. This is the
second twist.

Fergus is literally sick to his stomach with revulsion. The
third twist in the story comes at the end when Fergus, who
realizes that he's still in love with Dil, accepts her gender, even
though Fergus is heterosexual. The point, it seems, is that love
conquers all.

Endings

While twists can occur anywhere in a story, they typically
happen at the end. The classic TV series *The Twilight Zone* was
built around twist endings. In feature films, one of the most
famous twists in modern cinema was the ending of *The Sixth
Sense.* Another delicious twist ending occurs in the Spike Lee
film, *Inside Man.*

FILM EXAMPLES OF

TWISTS

CONTEMPORARY FILMS

Inside Man

Scene: Thief Dalton Russell (Clive Owen) walks out the front door
of the bank in broad daylight with the loot, just as he said he
would.

Twist: Russell hid in a false wall behind shelves in the bank's supply
room for a week until it was safe to leave.

Matchstick Men

Scene: Con artist Roy Waller (Nicolas Cage) awakens in a hospital bed. There's nobody around. Puzzled, he gets up, detaches himself from the monitors and exits.

Twist: Roy emerges and discovers that his "hospital room" is in a freight container on top of a parking garage. He realizes he's been conned out of his life savings by his partner, Frank (Sam Rockwell).

Phantom Thread

Scene: As their marriage once again teeters on dissolution, Alma (Vicky Krieps) makes an omelet and serves it to Reynolds (Daniel Day-Lewis). It's obvious that he knows that she has again used poisonous mushrooms to make him sick and completely reliant on her. We think he's going to sweep the plate off the table and banish her from his home. Instead, he stares at her, smiling, and begins to eat the omelet, knowing what it contains.

Twist: Having realized that she made him ill before and is about to do so again, Reynolds decides that he wants her to dominate and care for him, filling the emotional chasm left by the loss of his mother, whom he worshiped. Falling sick and allowing Alma to nurse him back to health will help to preserve their marriage, which they've both come to understand.

Shutter Island

Scene: At a mental institution on Shutter Island, US Marshal Teddy Daniels (Leonardo DiCaprio) is convinced that his partner Chuck Aule (Mark Ruffalo) is being held against his will. He breaks into the lighthouse where Dr. Cawley (Ben Kingsley) and Aule—who is actually Dr. Sheehan—are waiting for him.

Twist: Cawley and Sheehan tell Teddy that he's actually Andrew Laeddis, an inmate and convicted murder, and that the plot was an experiment in role play, hoping that it might cure Laeddis of his delusions.

Tully

Scene: After the birth of her third child, Marlo (Charlize Theron) struggles to cope, as her husband is constantly traveling for his job and she's often on her own. Her wealthy brother pays for a night nurse named Tully (Mackenzie Davis), who not only helps care for the newborn, but also helps Marlo emotionally.

After things get back on track, Tully deems her work done and departs.

Twist: It turns out that Tully is figment of Marlo's imagination, a younger version of herself that she has manifested in order to help her cope and come to terms with her life.

CLASSIC FILMS

Chinatown

Scene: Gittes (Jack Nicholson) tracks down Evelyn Mulwray (Faye Dunaway) and Katherine (Belinda Palmer) at a house in Santa Monica. He accuses Evelyn of murdering her husband, Hollis Mulwray (Darrell Zwerling), and holding Katherine, Mulray's mistress, hostage. Evelyn denies it all. Gittes demands the truth.

Twist: To Gittes's shock—as well as our own—Evelyn blurts out that Katherine is her sister AND her daughter, that is, that she was raped by her powerful and perverse father, Noah Cross (John Huston).

Terminator 2

Scene: Sarah Connor (Linda Hamilton) is in the middle of an escape attempt from a mental institution when the elevator doors part and out steps the Terminator (Arnold Schwarzenegger).

Twist: Unlike the first Terminator, this Terminator has been programmed to protect Sarah Connor and rather than try to harm her, instead it aids and abets her escape.

The Usual Suspects

Scene: Agent Dave Kujan (Chazz Palminteri) wraps up his interrogation of Roger "Verbal" Kint (Kevin Spacey) about a massacre aboard a ship and a plot masterminded by a criminal kingpin named Kaiser Söze. Kint, who has a limp and is meek and fearful, is granted his release without being charged.

Twist: After Kint leaves, Kujan looks at his bulletin board, which has names and places cited by Kint, and he realizes that everything Kint said was a fabrication made up on the spot using the bulletin board. Outside, as Kint walks toward his ride, his limp slowly melts away and we realize he's the infamous Kaiser Söze.

\\

Crisis / Black Moment

The final act

These next four chapters are linked, because taken together, they constitute the final leg of the story, which is Act III. Sometimes stuck screenwriters can get unstuck by heading directly here and thinking about the crisis (a.k.a. black moment), along with the ensuing action that leads to the confrontation (a.k.a. obligatory scene), climax (a.k.a. climax) and resolution (a.k.a. denouement). First let's start with the crisis.

All is lost

The crisis is the black moment where all looks lost in terms of the protagonist achieving their personal goal and/or their dramatic objective. Once again we need to be reminded that dramatic objective is distinct from personal goal and that it's possible for a character to attain their personal goal but not their dramatic objective (as well as vice versa).

To pull out of a crisis, something must occur that allows the protagonist to take one last kick at the can. It may be a decision that they make or it may be a new set of circumstances that they somehow create and use to resume their quest.

A new initiative

Once the protagonist undertakes this new initiative, it must be clear there's no turning back. Whatever action they've decided to undertake, it's a one-way trip. This new initiative moves us headlong into the first part of Act III.

The crisis can occur as a result of having something destroyed permanently. For example, in *The Godfather: Part II*, trust is destroyed when Michael realizes it was Fredo who betrayed the family, which resulted in the assassination of their brother Sonny. Michael is crushed by this revelation, because he knows what he now must do.

In *Gravity*, Ryan Stone has been fighting to survive pretty much the whole movie. Her crisis is when she finally gives up, turns off the oxygen in the *Soyuz* capsule and waits to die. She then hallucinates Kowalski and through him, convinces herself to live, or die trying. When she snaps back to reality, she decides to go for it.

Alternative crises

On the other hand, a crisis can be caused by something that's inherently positive. For example, you might have a protagonist who doesn't want to get tied down by a romantic relationship. He may have a dramatic objective that will have to be abandoned when he realizes he's madly in love which, in this case, would be his moment of crisis.

FILM EXAMPLES OF
CRISES

CONTEMPORARY FILMS

Ex Machina

Scene: Caleb (Domhnall Gleason) tells Nathan (Oscar Isaac) that he hacked the system the previous night when Nathan was drunk.

Crisis: This is the first moment that Nathan hasn't been in complete control, and he realizes he's been compromised, which could have dire consequences.

Get Out

Scene: Chris (Daniel Kaluuya) regains consciousness in the basement games room and realizes he's a prisoner. He then converses with Jim (Stephen Root) via a TV set and learns that Dean (Bradley Whitford) is going to transplant a part of Jim's brain into Chris in order to extend Jim's lifespan.

Crisis: Chris's worst fears are not just realized, but surpassed. He's not a prisoner of a white racist cult, but a white immortality cult that are going to use his body as a "vessel" in which Chris will retain consciousness but no will.

The King's Speech

Scene: Bertie (Colin Firth) has had a falling out with Logue (Geoffrey Rush) and is soon to be crowned king. After a meeting with the Accession Council in which his stammering returns, Bertie comes home and has an emotional breakdown.

Crisis: Bertie realizes the magnitude of the moment and that the love and support of his wife aren't enough; he realizes he must eat humble pie and reconcile with Logue.

The Martian

Scene: Mark (Matt Damon) is told that in order to reach escape velocity in the MAV, he will have to strip it down to almost nothing.

Crisis: Mark sends a message back: "Are you f***ing kidding me?" He knows the odds of this plan succeeding are infinitesimal.

Whiplash

Scene: At Fletcher's (J. K. Simmons) invitation, Andrew (Miles Teller) is set to play drums at the JVC Jazz Festival at Carnegie Hall, where influential record label reps are in the audience.

Crisis: Fletcher tricks Andrew by switching the repertoire. After aborted attempts to improvise, Andrew stops playing and walks off the stage, humiliated.

CLASSIC FILMS

Ordinary People

Scene: Conrad (Timothy Hutton) is at his grandparents' house at Christmas. He calls his friend Karen (Dinah Manoff), whom he met in the mental institution.

Crisis: Conrad is told by Karen's father that she committed suicide. Gripped by grief and despair, Conrad enters the bathroom and briefly contemplates suicide.

Tremors

Scene: Val (Kevin Bacon), Earl (Fred Ward), Rhonda (Finn Carter), and the others are stranded on a rocky outcrop, cornered by the surviving graboid (giant sandworm).

Crisis: The graboid has them right where it wants them. Eventually they'll have to leave the outcrop and make a run for it or they'll die of thirst. But if they run for it, they'll be completely exposed.

Working Girl

Scene: Katherine (Sigourney Weaver), corporate executive and Tess's (Melanie Griffith) horrible boss, bursts into a business meeting and exposes Tess as a fraud.

Crisis: Tess's dream of advancing in her career are dashed. She goes into a deep funk.

\\\\\\\\\\\\\\\\\\\\\\\\\\\\\\\\\\\\\

Confrontation / Obligatory Scene

Upon analysis, stuck writers might realize that their story lacks a confrontation. Armed with this knowledge, they can track back through the narrative and see whether they have set up the protagonist and antagonist in opposition. If not, they'll have to address the issue because inevitably the two must confront each other at this critical juncture.

Precursor to the climax

The confrontation is the precursor to the climax. As noted, the protagonist faces down the antagonist, whether it is another person or entity, the environment or nature, or the protagonist's own psychology or "inner demons."

Length

The confrontation is the direct result of the new initiative the protagonist takes following the crisis. In terms of its appropriate length, the confrontation can be brief or extended, but it's usually contained in one scene or a tight sequence leading to the climax.

Obliged

The confrontation is also referred to as the *obligatory scene* because, having set up and exploited for dramatic purposes the conflict between the protagonist and antagonist, we're now "obliged" to bring matters to a head, where one or the other will prevail. Not doing so will leave the story in limbo and the audience feeling incomplete.

FILM EXAMPLES OF
CONFRONTATION

CONTEMPORARY FILMS

Ex Machina
Scene: Nathan confronts Ava (Alicia Vikander) in the hallway.
Confrontation: They battle. Nathan destroys her arm with a metal rod. It seems like Nathan might prevail.

Get Out
Scene: Having thwarted the hypnosis-triggering teacup clink by stuffing cotton wadding in his ears, Chris endeavors to make his escape.
Confrontation: As he makes his escape, one by one, Chris is confronted by members of the immortality cult.

The King's Speech
Scene: With his country having just declared war on Germany, Bertie stands in the broadcasting booth and faces the dreaded BBC microphone.
Confrontation: The red light comes on and Bertie's throat tightens.

He looks over at Logue, who's calm. Bertie collects himself and begins.

The Martian

Scene: The MAV is launched. There are problems immediately: the tarp on the nose rips, slowing escape velocity. The *Ares* is going too fast, so they have to set off a bomb to slow down. The range between the *Ares* and Mark is beyond their limit. Commander Lewis (Jessica Chastain) detaches from her tether to work her way closer. In a last ditch maneuver, Mark uses a knife to slit his spacesuit glove so it will rapidly expel oxygen and propel him closer to Lewis.

Confrontation: Mark and the crew of the *Ares* face off against their unforgiving adversary: outer space.

Whiplash

Scene: Andrew returns onstage to the drums and starts playing. The band joins him in a rendition of the song "Caravan."

Confrontation: Fletcher is near apoplectic and tries to stop Andrew, who ignores him and keeps playing, really sticking it to Fletcher.

CLASSIC FILMS

Ordinary People

Scene: Conrad runs into the street, his mind flashing back to the boating accident where his older brother perished. He calls Dr. Berger (Judd Hirsch) and they agree to meet at his office.

Confrontation: Conrad confesses that he feels responsible for the death of his brother and Berger helps him grapple with his guilt. Conrad faces his inner demons.

Tremors

Scene: They throw a pipe bomb at the graboid, which swallows it and then spits it out. It lands on the rocky outcrop and they all run for cover. Val, Earl, and Rhonda find themselves fifty yards from the rocky outcrop, exposed.

Confrontation: The graboid begins to stalk them, shoving earth upward to make them lose their balance so it can triangulate their location from the sound of their feet. If they move, they'll be eaten alive. Advantage: graboid.

Working Girl

Scene: Tess packs up her desk and goes to the elevator. Jack (Harrison Ford) arrives. So does Katherine, who accuses her of stealing. Tess calls her a liar.

Confrontation: Vying for Jack's affections, the two women confront each other. Katherine feigns outrage, while Tess bravely stands her ground.

32

///

Climax

The climax is the moment of truth. It often incorporates a final decision. The protagonist must decide whether to turn tail and run or face down the antagonist. It also answers the "great questions" posed at the start of the story, which are "Will the protagonist attain their dramatic objective?" and "Will the protagonist realize their personal goal?"

Questions posed

For example, in *Rocky*, the great questions are "Will Rocky go the distance (dramatic objective) and prove that he's not just a bum (personal goal)?" In *The Devil's Advocate*, the great questions are "Will Kevin Lomax reject his satanic birthright and all its prerequisites (dramatic objective), and in so doing, prove that he's not evil (personal goal)?"

Scope

The climax of a story can be big and loud, as the word itself suggests, or it can be small in scope, even wordless, if that would be more organic to the style of the story.

For example, in *The Remains of the Day*, the butler Stevens has one last chance to profess his love for Mrs. Kenton, but he just can't bring himself to do it and instead watches silently as the bus departs and carries her out of his life forever. Emotionally, the moment is huge and tragic. Onscreen, we see a man in quiet turmoil watching a bus pull away.

FILM EXAMPLES OF
CLIMAXES

CONTEMPORARY FILMS

Ex Machina

Scene: Still in the hallway, Nathan is stabbed in the back by Kyoko (Sonoya Mizuno), then in the front by Ava.

Climax: Surprised that this is going to be the outcome of his "experiment," Nathan collapses and dies.

Get Out

Scene: Chris dispatches Rose (Allison Williams), Jeremy (Caleb Landry Jones), Dean, then Missy (Catherine Keener), then Georgina (Betty Gabriel), then Walter (Marcus Henderson), then Jeremy again. The police arrive on the scene.

Climax: Chris survives and the members of the cult are destroyed.

The King's Speech

Scene: With Logue nearby for support, Bertie reads the speech on the radio.

Climax: Bertie prevails over his stammer and his fear (and by implication, over his cruel, overbearing father).

The Martian

Scene: Commander Lewis and Mark approach each other and make contact. She's able to hold onto him. He's going to survive.

Climax: Mark (with the support of the other astronauts) has survived being marooned on Mars.

Whiplash

Scene: The song ends, but Andrew continues playing a drum solo with exceptional virtuosity.

Climax: Fletcher realizes that Andrew is the gifted student he's long sought. Energized, he resumes conducting.

CLASSIC FILMS

Ordinary People

Scene: Conrad role-plays with Dr. Berger as his mind flashes back to the boating accident where his brother Buck died.

Climax: With Dr. Berger's help, Conrad has an epiphany that his only "sin" was being stronger than his older brother. Conrad finally lets go of his guilt. In so doing, he vanquishes his demons.

Tremors

Scene: Val gets an idea. Gripping the last pipe bomb, he starts running, followed by Earl and Rhonda. The graboid gives chase. Val lights the pipe bomb and throws it behind the graboid, where it explodes. The graboid is forced to speed up and crashes through the side of the cliff, plummeting to its death.

Climax: Val outsmarts the graboid by getting the idea to cause what he endearingly calls a "stampede."

Working Girl

Scene: Jack ushers Trask (Philip Bosco) and Tess into an elevator, where she explains how she came up with the idea to buy Metro. When they exit the elevator, Trask asks Katherine how *she* came up with the idea. Katherine comes up empty, exposing her lies.

Climax: Through Trask, Tess puts Katherine on the spot. When it becomes clear that Katherine is a liar, Trask tells her to get her "bony ass" out of his sight. By winning Trask over, Tess prevails over her horrible boss.

\\\

Resolution / Denouement

The resolution is the outcome of the climax. The questions about the protagonist's personal goal and dramatic objective have been answered. The protagonist has undergone character growth. The situation is irrevocably changed from how it was in the beginning of the story. The resolution dots all the i's and crosses all the t's and suggests how the characters' lives will carry on after the final FADE OUT.

A final twist

The resolution can sometimes incorporate a final twist. For example, in *Parenthood*, a child is born and we assume it belongs to Julie, since she was pregnant when last seen onscreen. But then Julie is then shown holding her own baby, and it's revealed that the newborn belongs to her mother, Karen, who married Mr. Bowman.

Length

Typically the resolution is short—one or two pages. We've all seen films where we thought the story was over but the narrative kept on going. Or films that had too many endings, which has the same effect. Ideally, resolutions should be as brief as possible.

~~~~~~

FILM EXAMPLES OF

RESOLUTIONS

CONTEMPORARY FILMS

Ex Machina

Scene: Ava is glimpsed standing on a busy street corner.

Resolution: This may be the beginning of the end for humankind.

Get Out

Scene: Back in the present, Chris is visited in prison by his friend Rod (Lil Rel Howery). Chris can't remember the names of the people he killed, whose bodies were consumed by a fire that destroyed the mansion.

Resolution: Even though Chris is the victim, he's in jail because a Black man can't murder a bunch of white folks without the presumption of guilt by the justice system. And yet Chris is at peace, having thwarted the cult, thereby saving the lives of future victims.

The King's Speech

Scene: Bertie and his family walk out onto the balcony to wave to their hordes of cheering subjects.

Resolution: Bertie is going to make an excellent king.

The Martian

Scene: Mark is back on Earth, savoring its hospitable climate. In a NASA lecture theater, he addresses a group of astronaut recruits.

Resolution: A living legend, Mark will continue to serve as an example that the difference between life and death in outer space is just a matter of solving problems.

Whiplash

Scene: The band joins in a final fanfare. Fletcher is blown away by Andrew, while his dad, Jim (Paul Reiser), is stunned by what his son has become.

Resolution: Because of his "trial by fire," Andrew may become a jazz great, but we are left wondering at what personal cost.

CLASSIC FILMS

Ordinary People

Scene: Beth (Mary Tyler Moore) finds Calvin (Donald Sutherland) crying in the garage. He says their marriage is over. Stunned, Beth leaves in a taxi. Conrad and Calvin comfort each other.

Resolution: Conrad has finally found some peace. Beth and Calvin separate and will likely get divorced. The writing has been on the wall for some time. Conversely, the bond between Calvin and Conrad has been strengthened.

Tremors

Scene: The road has reopened and Val and Earl are preparing to leave town as per their original plan. Rhonda thanks them for saving her life and walks to her truck.

Resolution: Earl can read Rhonda's signals, and he nudges Val to do something about it. Despite his feelings of inferiority, Val catches up to Rhonda, and before he can speak, they embrace and kiss.

Working Girl

Scene: Tess arrives for her first day of work at Trask Industries.

Resolution: Tess learns that she's been hired as an executive, not a secretary.

34

Emotion

It's not that I haven't already alluded to this topic; I just want to give it a little bit more emphasis. Mastering all the tools, techniques, and craft in this book will mean nothing if your audience doesn't *feel* something. You have to touch their heart, or quicken their pulse, or tickle their funny bone, or stir them to action. Win hearts, win minds.

I often reflect on the following film moments that have moved me:

- The overwhelming joy and gut-wrenching remorse of the decision Jim Preston makes to rouse Aurora Lane from suspended animation in the film *Passengers*.
- The side-splitting "ludes kick in" sequence in *Wolf of Wall Street*.
- The unexpected ending of *Phantom Thread*, where Reynolds Woodcock knowingly eats an omelet prepared by his wife that's laced with poisonous mushrooms.

- The climactic scene in which Dr. Sean Maguire repeatedly says "It's not your fault" to Will Hunting in *Good Will Hunting*.

- Patient Leonard Lowe, in the throes of a seizure, tells Dr. Sayer to film him and "Learn, learn learn!" in *Awakenings*.

- Ray Kinsella asks his young dad, "You wanna have a catch?" in *Field of Dreams*.

- Ted Stroehmann gets his private parts caught in his zipper in *There's Something About Mary*. The police and fire department arrive and announce, "We got a bleeder!"

- After incredible hardship, the two dogs Luath and Bodger and the cat Tao miraculously reunite with young Peter at the end of *The Incredible Journey*.

- A single tear rolls down surgeon Frederick Treves's cheek when he first sets eyes on the grotesque John Merrick in *The Elephant Man*.

- Frankie tells Maggie that *mo cuishle* means "my darling and my blood" before he compassionately euthanizes her in *Million Dollar Baby*.

- AIDS-afflicted Andrew Beckett listens to Maria Callas sing the aria *La Moma Morta,* and at the climax says, "I am Love" in *Philadelphia*.

- In *To Kill a Mockingbird,* Atticus Finch prepares to exit the courtroom after defending Tom Robinson in a lost cause. In the segregated balcony above, his daughter Scout sits with the town's Black citizens. They all rise out of respect and Mr. Sykes says to Scout, "Miss Jean Louise. Stand up. Your father's passing."

The above moments come from stories that address topics such as child abuse, disease, faith, love, compassion, euthanasia, grace, and racism. We remember how these films made us feel and because of this, we remember what they had to say. They resonate.

American film director Howard Hawks once said that a good movie is "three good scenes and no bad ones." As screenwriters, we should be so lucky to be inspired to create characters or pen scenes or write dialogue that one day might become iconic.

\\

Practical Advice

Circling back to the musical analogy I used in the preface to this book, if you've ever had any lessons on a musical instrument, you'll recall that one of the techniques you had to learn was "fingering."

Oh, get your mind out of the gutter—it just means which finger is used to play which note. Or you may have heard a beginner play an instrument haltingly. It's largely because they're trying to remember which finger goes where. Plink, plink.

Musical technique is analogous to screenwriting craft in that until you get to the point when it's second nature—in other words, where it's *integrated*—the playing of the music and the writing of the screenplay will be laborious. And to be honest—not heaps of fun.

So what I'm saying is that the knowledge you've gained from this book is going to make the writing process a bit arduous in the short term. The free-form creativity that you once enjoyed is going to be replaced with a lot of pausing and thinking about screenwriting craft as you write. It won't feel much like a creative endeavor for a while. I'm sorry!

But take heart, because there's a pony among all the manure. Like a dedicated musician who practices to the point where their technique is automatic, so too will it be for the screenwriter who writes every day. Your craft will soon become second nature. Free-form creativity will once again return, this time solidly underpinned by craft.

When this happens for musicians, they're on their way to virtuosity—assuming they have talent and remain disciplined. Screenwriters will find the same thing happening; your writing will go faster, the results will be better, and the process will be fun again.

Virtuosity is the integration of craft and creativity. Many musicians and writers report that while playing or writing, they "disappear," often losing track of time. Hours pass like minutes. They say that it's like the music or story is being channeled through them.

These are known as "peak experiences" and they'll be available to you too once you've mastered your craft so thoroughly that you don't consciously think about it while you're writing. It's a state of grace, and when you achieve it, there's no better high.

To outline or not to outline

Some screenwriters work everything out in their head before setting a word to paper. Others sit down and start writing in a stream of consciousness kind of way without knowing beforehand how the story is going to resolve until they arrive there.

If you successfully employ one of these techniques, I hate you. I mean, uh, good on you. Go for it. Most of us blue-collar screenwriters need to "beat out" the story, meaning that we identify the act breaks, plot points, and ending in order to craft an **outline** before we start working on a draft. In television, this process often happens in a group and is called "breaking the story."

Whatever the terminology, the idea here is that before adding dialogue, we work out the basic structure of the narrative. We then expand this into a scene-by-scene description of the story, written in discrete paragraphs. The resulting document is called a "**treatment**."

Once your treatment is bulletproof, it's time to go to **first draft** by adding dialogue. This process not only helps to first solve the structure, it also forces us to write visually—to use description to tell as much of the story as possible without relying on dialogue.

Writing is rewriting and rewriting and rewriting and rewriting and rewriting

You've heard that writing is rewriting. It was true for me in the creation of this book and it's been true for every screenplay or teleplay I've ever penned. That said, for many writers, facing the blank page and getting something down can be a big challenge.

The reasons are manifold. We feel uninspired. We come up blank. We doubt our talent. If we do manage to get something written, what ends up on the page doesn't reflect what we had in our mind's eye. We fret and obsess that what we've written isn't very good.

Please note: this happens to almost *every writer*. The difference between those who go on to finish screenplays and those who abandon their efforts is the knowledge and belief that comes from knowing *experientially* that all material improves through rewriting.

Start small

It's one thing to describe this process, but another to grasp it without having personal experience. So consider this suggestion: start small. Don't try to write a feature-length screenplay right away. Instead, write short screenplays, perhaps a half-hour in length.

Don't worry at this juncture whether you'll be able to sell a stand-alone half-hour screenplay. The end game here isn't to sell the script; it's to finish it. It's much easier to get to the end of a first draft that you're insecure about if it's only twenty-four pages long.

Progress

Let's say you push on through and get to the end. Congrats! The work is raw, but this is where the magic begins. You read it over and you start getting new ideas. Better ideas. You may not have solutions for all the problems, but you're starting to make progress.

You undertake a rewrite, incorporating your new and improved ideas. You get to the end again because *it's only twenty-four pages long* and therefore attainable. Now you should leave it alone for a few weeks. Do some additional research, if necessary. Take in a ballgame.

Multiple drafts

After a decent interval, reread it and you'll come up with ideas for the areas that are still deficient and perhaps some newer ideas to improve upon the last set of ideas. This is the process.

Be prepared to write three, five or ten drafts of the screenplay if need be.

This first-hand experience of seeing the work improve through rewriting will give you the insight to know that every work has raw beginnings and it will help you keep going when your initial drafts inevitably come up short. This is how it works. Every time.

Once you have this understanding, then and only then should you consider tackling longer formats. The next screenplay you write might be forty-eight pages long, like a one-hour television pilot. Get to the end. Rewrite multiple times. Once you're satisfied that you grasp the process, then you can attempt to write a feature-length screenplay.

The inmates take over the asylum

There will be a moment when you're rewriting when you'll have this thought: "he/she wouldn't do/say that." What's happening is that your characters are beginning to dictate their actions. No longer can you force them to do or say things that are out of character. They won't allow it. They're starting to become more dimensional. This is good.

Character is plot

Up to this point, you've been manipulating your characters like marionettes at the service of the plot. But no more. Now they'll start dictating the plot, behaving like rebellious children. Don't be a controlling parent! You *want* this to happen, just as we want our own real-life children to become independent. You might have to toss out some material that no longer tracks, but again like real-life parenting, all the sacrifices are worth it.

Not a quaff

You're now moving toward a mature draft, which doesn't mean a nicely aged beer, but rather a screenplay that's undergone a lot of revision and has started to take on a life of its own. When you get to the point where you've done multiple drafts and can't come up with any more improvements, it's time to seek a third-party critique.

Who should give input

A critique should be provided by someone who can be objective, which disqualifies spouses, partners, family, and friends. If you don't know anyone who's knowledgeable about screenwriting that can provide constructive criticism, join a screenwriters group.

Members of a screenwriters group critique each other's material. No money is involved, except perhaps for donations to buy snacks for in-person meetings. The amount of experience of the screenwriters in the group will determine the quality of the feedback, so try to find people who are either at or slightly above your level.

Receiving notes

Some notes will be brilliant, and you'll wonder how you didn't think of them first. Be glad for these gems and lavish praise upon the person who furnished them. Conversely, other notes will be completely useless, as the person either didn't get what you were trying to achieve or, for whatever reason, was unable to set aside their own subjectivity.

If this happens, no matter how inane the notes, don't debate them, as you don't want to be seen as defensive (i.e., "difficult"). If there are notes you don't agree with, politely ask for "clarification." Sometimes the explanation will reveal a deficiency that *does* need to be addressed, and with further thought, you'll devise a better, more palatable solution.

Story consulting

Another option is to hire a qualified **story consultant**. These are pros who provide written notes (and perhaps also a phone, Internet, or in-person meeting to go over the notes). Most have websites that describe their background and experience. As with anyone you hire, it's always a good idea to check references and be clear about price and terms.

Competition

As already noted, musicians practice and composers compose for years before they're good enough to be paid for their work. Furthermore, they continue to practice on a daily basis to remain masters of their craft. And as with any creative field, there's competition.

The "wunderkind"

From time to time you'll hear that some young Turk had their first script bought or produced by a major studio. Not only did they get paid big bucks, they're now being sought by all the major players. Feelings of envy may arise, followed by despair.

Suck it up. It happens—like winning the lottery happens, with the odds being about the same. It's very rare that someone sells (not just options, which is quite common) their first screenplay, so when it happens it tends to get ink, as it makes good copy.

The point in mentioning this is that you shouldn't be disheartened. First, a new and unknown writer breaking through means that this possibility is available to you as well. Second, I've observed that more often than not, the wunderkind is a one-hit wonder.

If I may be permitted to allude to the tortoise and hare fable, if you just keep plugging away and developing your skills, you'll have career success. What's more, because your foundation (craft) is solid and your approach is professional, you'll also have longevity.

Hunkering down

So you need to hunker down for the long haul. Accept the fact that you may have to write multiple screenplays before you get any interest in your work. And the first offers may be to write for very little money or to write works for hire based on supplied ideas. That's okay.

Be prolific

Let's mine one last nugget out of our musical analogy. Have you ever encountered a new recording artist's work—whether it be on the radio, online, or some other media—and you liked what you heard, so you checked out their body of work?

You may have discovered the song you liked was from the artist's *fifth* album. In other words, the artist had already recorded four albums before their music bubbled up to your attention. You can well imagine how much work this entailed, how many hours.

What lesson does this hold for a screenwriter? Be prolific. Keep turning out new work. Every screenplay you write will be better than the previous one and it will help you to not only develop your craft, but your own distinctive voice as well. The more work you have out there garnering positive notices, the closer you'll be to achieving critical mass.

Ultimately nothing is wasted, because if you break through with your fifth (or tenth) screenplay, producers and agents will ask to see what you have "in the drawer." You'll dust these screenplays off, polish them up, and send them back out. The material will be read with new and more receptive eyes. Yes, *more receptive*. Let me explain.

Perception and acceptance

How people evaluate material is affected by how they perceive it beforehand. If the consensus is that something's going to be good, it often gets the benefit of the doubt. It's human nature. Psychologically, there's a group mentality at work. In show business, this is called "acceptance," and for an artist, it's the equivalent of the Holy Grail.

In live stand-up comedy, acceptance is something that comedians can experience in real time. When starting out, unknown comics walk onstage and the audience's attitude is "go ahead, try to make me laugh." They're initially skeptical; that is, they're a tough crowd.

On the other hand, more seasoned comics who have already earned acceptance walk onstage and make a signature gesture or facial expression and the audience howls. Folks are onside before the comic tells the first joke. *This* is the power of acceptance.

As an emerging screenwriter, your work will be read through the reader's perception that you're a newbie, so similar to a "tough crowd," they'll be skeptical. Your material will have to be good enough to trump their "show me" attitude. Also, the reader's ass is on the line, so they won't recommend anything marginal, as that would be an unnecessary risk.

Conversely, if the general consensus is that you're the next big thing or the last film you wrote was a commercial success, readers will evaluate your screenplay through the lens that you're a talented, proven writer. They'll look forward to the read. They'll lean in your direction. They don't want to be lone naysayers. This is acceptance.

When I was chasing my first screenwriting jobs, my agent told me that I'd have to write an Oscar or Emmy quality screenplay as my calling card in order to get people to take a chance and hire me. He went on to say that once I started getting jobs, I'd never have to write that well again! He was joking, of course, but there's a grain of truth there.

Karma and luck

My take on karma and luck is that you make your own. If you sit around waiting for the proverbial phone to ring, it won't. But if you're busy writing, submitting, and networking, it more likely will. The same thing goes for luck. Lucky people are those who are active. They're in the right place at the right time because they've taken the initiative to be there.

Marketing and self-promotion

In other words, nothing just shows up. You have to

1. Market yourself online in every way possible
2. Network *in person* with your peers and potential employers at every opportunity
3. Use any appropriate means or path available to get your work out there and read

Timing

Having said all that, even if your script is perfect, it still has to arrive in exactly the right hands at exactly the right time. Whoever is reading it either knows what they're seeking or they know what the person they work for is seeking. And hopefully it's your script.

However, to use an astronomical term, if your work is outside the "habitable zone," then regardless of its quality, it won't make the cut. If you (or your agent) have access to market intelligence so you can make targeted submissions, that would give you an edge. Short of that, you have to use a shotgun strategy and be prepared for copious rejection.

Catch-22

In order to be perceived as a pro, you need produced credits. On the other hand, you don't want to accept work that's unexciting and/or doesn't meet your standards, no matter how much you want a screen credit or need the money. So what's the solution?

Be true to thyself

Do the work that gives you the most joy in terms of creative fulfillment. You'll be happier doing work that you love. Cream always rises to the top, so if your work has merit, you'll eventually break through and all the other good stuff will follow.

Accept all invitations

This is something of a life lesson for me. Unless I have a conflict, I rarely say no to an invitation. You can't predict where life's going to take you, but it won't take you very far unless you're open to possibilities. Who might you meet? You never know.

Confidence

Unless you collaborate with a partner, writing is a solitary endeavor. The temperament required isn't necessarily one that's associated with extroversion. Networking events and pitch meetings can be awkward. They certainly were for me early in my career.

Compounding things is the fact that you don't yet have a lot of evidence (screen credits, produced work) to prove that you should be considered a professional writer. If people sense your lack of confidence, interactions can be uncomfortable and unsuccessful.

How do you garner confidence before you're "legit"? It's simple. *Write every day.* As with any endeavor, discipline builds confidence. It says to you and others that you're not a dabbler. You're serious. In short order, confidence will no longer be an issue.

It's your movie

Art imitates life, life imitates art. If you were to come up with a premise for your life, what would it be? It might change as you age, but what would it be *right now*? Your life is your personal movie and it's up to you to live it fully, as you can't count on there being a sequel. Like your characters, be proactive and don't let anything stand in your way.

Success

Whatever success looks like for you, I hope you achieve it. And if one day a fan approaches you and says that something you wrote "moved them deeply" or "changed their life" or "inspired them to become a writer," you'll feel satisfied that all the effort, doubt, and perseverance to get yourself unstuck was worth it. Good luck!

LIST OF FILMS DISCUSSED

CLASSIC FILMS

A Clockwork Orange
Screenplay by Stanley Kubrick based on the novel *A Clockwork Orange* by Anthony Burgess

A Few Good Men
Written by Aaron Sorkin based on his stage play *A Few Good Men*

A Perfect Murder
Screenplay by Patrick Smith Kelly based on the stage play *Dial M for Murder* by Frederick Knott

A Streetcar Named Desire
Screenplay by Tennessee Williams and adaptation by Oscar Saul based on the stage play *A Streetcar Named Desire* by Tennessee Williams

Airplane
Written for the Screen by Jim Abrahams & David Zucker & Jerry Zucker

Alien
Screenplay by Dan O'Bannon based on a story by Dan O'Bannon and Ronald Shusett

All the President's Men
Screenplay by William Goldman based on the book *All the President's Men* by Carl Bernstein and Bob Woodward

Amadeus
Screenplay by Peter Shaffer based on his stage play *Amadeus*

Annie Hall
Written by Woody Allen and Marshall Brickman

Apocalypse Now
Written by John Milius and Francis Ford Coppola

Apollo 13
Screenplay by William Broyles Jr. and Al Reinert based on the book *Lost Moon* by Jim Lovell and Jeffrey Kluger

Awakenings
Screenplay by Steven
Zaillian based on the book
Awakenings by Oliver Sacks

Being There
Written by Jerzy Kosinksi
based on his novel *Being There*

Big
Written by Gary Ross and
Anne Spielberg

The Big Lebowski
Written by Ethan Coen and
Joel Coen

Blade Runner
Written by Hampton Fancher
and David Webb Peoples
based on the novel *Do
Androids Dream of Electric
Sheep?* by Philip K. Dick

**The Bridge on the River
Kwai**
Written by Carl Foreman and
Michael Wilson based on the
novel *The Bridge over the River
Kwai* by Pierre Boulle

Bugsy
Written by James Toback
based on the book by Dean
Jennings

Casino
Screenplay by Nicholas Pileggi
& Martin Scorsese based on
the book *Casino* by Nicholas
Pileggi

Charly
Screenplay by Stirling
Silliphant based on the novel
Flowers for Algernon by Daniel
Keyes

The China Syndrome
Written by Mike Gray & T. S.
Cook and James Bridges

Chinatown
Written by Robert Towne

City Slickers
Written by Lowell Ganz &
Babaloo Mandel

**Close Encounters of the
Third Kind**
Written by Steven Spielberg

Coming to America
Screenplay by David Sheffield
& Barry W. Blaustein; story by
Eddie Murphy

The Crying Game
Written by Neil Jordan

Dances with Wolves
Screenplay by Michael Blake
based on his novel *Dances
with Wolves*

Dave
Written by Gary Ross

Dead Man Walking
Written by Tim Robbins based
on the book by Sister Helen
Prejean

Dead Poets Society
Written by Tom Schulman

The Devil's Advocate
Screenplay by Jonathan
Lemkin and Tony Gilroy
based on the novel *The
Devil's Advocate* by Andrew
Neiderman

DOA
Story and Screenplay by Russell
Rouse and Clarence Greene

Dog Day Afternoon
Screenplay by Frank Pierson

The Elephant Man
Screenplay by Christopher De
Vore & Eric Bergren & David
Lynch based on the books
*The Elephant Man and Other
Reminiscences* by Sir Frederick
Treves and *The Elephant Man:
A Study in Human Dignity* by
Ashley Montagu

Enemy Mine
Screenplay by Edward Khmara
based on the story *Enemy
Mine* by Barry Longyear

Enemy of the State
Written by David Marconi

The Exorcist
Written by William Peter Blatty
based on his novel *The Exorcist*

Field of Dreams
Screenplay by Phil Alden
Robinson based on the book
Shoeless Joe by W. P. Kinsella

Fight Club
Screenplay by Jim Uhls based
on the novel *Fight Club* by
Check Palahniuk

The Fly
Screenplay by Charles Edward
Pogue and David Cronenberg
based on the short story "The
Fly" by George Langelaan

Forrest Gump
Screenplay by Eric Roth based
on the novel *Forrest Gump* by
Winston Groom

Frankenstein
Screenplay by Garrett Fort and
Francis Edward Faragoh based

on the novel *Frankenstein* by
Mary Shelley

The Fugitive
Screenplay by Jeb Stuart and
David Twohy based on a story
by David Twohy

The Full Monty
Written by Simon Beaufoy

Gandhi
Written by John Briley

Ghostbusters
Written by Dan Aykroyd and
Harold Ramis

The Godfather
Screenplay by Francis Ford
Coppola and Mario Puzo
based on the novel *The
Godfather* by Mario Puzo

The Godfather: Part II
Screenplay by Francis Ford
Coppola and Mario Puzo
based on the novel *The
Godfather* by Mario Puzo

Going in Style
Screenplay by Martin Brest
based on a story by Edward
Cannon

Good Will Hunting
Written by Matt Damon and
Ben Affleck

Groundhog Day
Screenplay by Danny Rubin
and Harold Ramis based on a
story by Danny Rubin

Harold and Maude
Written by Colin Higgins

Heathers
Written by Daniel Waters

Hell in the Pacific
Screenplay by Alexander
Jacobs and Eric Bercovici
based on a story by Reuben
Bercovitch

High Noon
Written by Carl Foreman
based on the short story
"The Tin Star" by John W.
Cunningham

Home Alone
Written by John Hughes

The Incredible Journey
Screenplay by James Algar
based on the book *The
Incredible Journey* by Sheila
Burnford

The Insider
Written by Eric Roth & Michael
Mann based on the article
"The Man Who Knew Too
Much" by Marie Brenner

Invasion of the Body
Snatchers
Screenplay by W. D. Richter
based on the novel *The Body
Snatchers* by Jack Finney

It's a Wonderful Life
Screenplay by Frances
Goodrich & Albert Hackett
and Frank Capra based on the
short story "The Greatest Gift"
by Philip Van Doren Stern

Jerry Maguire
Written by Cameron Crowe

The Last Emperor
Screenplay by Mark Peploe
with Bernardo Bertolucci

Lawrence of Arabia
Screenplay by Robert Bold
and Michael Wilson based
on *Seven Pillars of Wisdom* by
T. E. Lawrence

Little Big Man
Screenplay by Calder
Willingham based on the
novel *Little Big Man* by Thomas
Berger

Lorenzo's Oil
Written by George Miller and
Nick Enright

Mad Max
Screenplay by James
McCausland & George Miller
based on a story by George
Miller and Byron Kennedy

Malcolm X
Screenplay by Arnold Perl
and Spike Lee based on *The
Autobiography of Malcolm X* by
Alex Haley and Malcolm X

The Maltese Falcon
Screenplay by John Huston
based on the novel *The
Maltese Falcon* by Dashiell
Hammett

Manhattan
Written by Woody Allen and
Marshall Brickman

The Mask
Screenplay by Mike Werb;
story by Michael Fallon and
Mark Verheiden

The Matrix
Written by The Wachowskis

Midnight Cowboy
Screenplay by Waldo Salt
based on the novel *Midnight
Cowboy* by James Leo Herlihy

Moby Dick
Screenplay by Ray Bradbury
and John Huston based on the
novel *Moby-Dick* by Herman
Melville

Mrs. Doubtfire
Screenplay by Randi Mayem
Singer and Leslie Dixon based
on the novel *Alias Madame
Doubtfire* by Anne Fine

The Natural
Screenplay by Roger Towne
and Phil Dusenberry based
on the novel *The Natural* by
Bernard Malamud

Notting Hill
Written by Richard Curtis

The Odd Couple
Written by Neil Simon based
on his stage play *The Odd
Couple*

One Flew Over the Cuckoo's Nest
Screenplay by Lawrence
Hauben and Bo Goldman
based on the novel *One Flew
Over the Cuckoo's Nest* by Ken
Kesey

Ordinary People
Screenplay by Alvin Sargent
based on the novel *Ordinary
People* by Judith Guest

Outbreak
Written by Laurence Dworet
and Robert Roy Pool

Outland
Written by Peter Hyams

Papillion
Screenplay by Dalton Trumbo
and Lorenzo Semple Jr. based

on the book *Papillon* by Henri
Charrière

Parenthood
Screenplay by Lowell Ganz
and Babaloo Mandel based
on a story by Lowell Ganz,
Babaloo Mandel, and Ron
Howard

Philadelphia
Written by Ron Nyswaner

The Player
Screenplay by Michael Tolkin
based on his novel *The Player*

Pretty Woman
Written by J. F. Lawton

Quiz Show
Screenplay by Paul
Attanasio based on the book
*Remembering America: A Voice
from the Sixties* by Richard N.
Goodwin

Raiders of the Lost Ark
Screenplay by Lawrence
Kasdan; story by George Lucas
and Philip Kaufman

Rain Man
Screenplay by Ronald Bass
and Barry Morrow based on a
story by Barry Morrow

The Remains of the Day
Screenplay by Ruth Prawer
Jhabvala based on the novel
The Remains of the Day by
Kazuo Ishiguro

Rocky
Written by Sylvester Stallone

Romeo and Juliet
Screenplay by Franco Brusati
& Masolino D'Amico & Franco

Zeffirelli based on the stage play *Romeo and Juliet* by William Shakespeare

Rudy
Written by Angelo Pizzo

Saturday Night Fever
Screenplay by Norman Wexler based on the magazine article "Tribal Rites of the New Saturday Night" by Nik Cohn

Scarface
Screenplay by Oliver Stone

Schindler's List
Screenplay by Steven Zaillian based on the book *Schindler's List* by Thomas Keneally

The Shawshank Redemption
Screenplay by Frank Darabont based on the short story "Rita Hayworth and Shawshank Redemption" by Stephen King

The Sixth Sense
Written by M. Night Shyamalan

The Terminator
Written by James Cameron and Gale Anne Hurd

Terminator 2: Judgment Day
Written by James Cameron & William Wisher

Terms of Endearment
Screenplay by James L. Brooks based on the novel *Terms of Endearment* by Larry McMurtry

There's Something About Mary
Screenplay by Ed Decter & John J. Strauss and Peter Farrelly & Bobby Farrelly; story by Ed Decter & John J. Strauss

The Time Machine
Screenplay by David Duncan based on the novel *The Time Machine* by H. G. Wells

To Kill a Mockingbird
Screenplay by Horton Foote based on the novel *To Kill a Mockingbird* by Harper Lee

Tootsie
Screenplay by Larry Gelbart & Murray Schisgal based on a story by Don McGuire and Larry Gelbart

Toy Story 2
Screenplay by Andrew Stanton and Rita Hsiao and Doug Chamberlin & Chris Webb; original story by John Lasseter & Pete Docter & Ash Brannon & Andrew Stanton

Tremors
Screenplay by S. S. Wilson & Brent Maddock; story by S. S. Wilson & Brent Maddock & Ron Underwood

Tucker: The Man and His Dream
Written by Arnold Schulman and David Seidler

12 Monkeys
Screenplay by David Webb Peoples and Janet Peoples

Twister
Written by Michael Chrichton
& Anne-Marie Martin

2001: A Space Odyssey
Screenplay by Stanley Kubrick
and Arthur C. Clarke based on
the short story "The Sentinel"
by Arthur C. Clarke

The Usual Suspects
Written by Christopher
McQuarrie

Wall Street
Written by Stanley Weiser &
Oliver Stone

West Side Story
Screenplay by Ernest Lehman
based on the musical stage
play by Jerome Robbins,
Leonard Bernstein, Stephen
Sondheim, and Arthur
Laurents

When Harry Met Sally
Written by Nora Ephron

Working Girl
Written by Kevin Wade

CONTEMPORARY FILMS

A Beautiful Mind
Written by Akiva Goldsman
based on the book *A Beautiful
Mind* by Sylvia Nasar

A Quiet Place
Screenplay by Bryan Woods &
Scott Beck and John Krasinski;
story by Bryan Woods & Scott
Beck

About a Boy
Screenplay by Peter Hedges,
Chris Weitz & Paul Weitz based
on the novel *About a Boy* by
Nick Hornby

American Made
Written by Gary Spinelli

Avatar
Written by James Cameron

Bad Words
Written by Andrew Dodge

Big Fish
Screenplay by John August

based on the novel *Big Fish: A
Novel of Mythic Proportions* by
Daniel Wallace

The Big Short
Screenplay by Charles
Randolph and Adam McKay
based on the book *The Big
Short* by Michael Lewis

The Big Sick
Written by Emily V. Gordon
and Kumail Nanjiani

The Blind Side
Written by John Lee Hancock
based on the book *The Blind
Side: Evolution of a Game* by
Michael Lewis

The Bucket List
Written by Justin Zackham

Captain Phillips
Screenplay by Billy Ray based
on the book *A Captain's
Duty* by Richard Phillips and
Stephan Talty

Cast Away
Written by William Broyles Jr.

Catch Me If You Can
Screenplay by Jeff Nathanon based on the book *Catch Me If You Can* by Frank Abagnale Jr. and Stan Redding

Children of Men
Screenplay by Alfonso Cuarón & Timothy J. Sexton and David Arata and Mark Fergus & Hawk Ostby based on the novel *The Children of Men* by P. D. James

The Cooler
Written by Frank Hannah & Wayne Kramer

Dallas Buyers Club
Written by Craig Borten and Melisa Wallack

Dawn of the Planet of the Apes
Written by Mark Bomback and Rick Jaffa & Amanda Silver based on characters created by Rick Jaffa & Amanda Silver

Deadpool
Written by Rhett Reese and Paul Wernick

The Devil Wears Prada
Screenplay by Aline Brosh McKenna based on the novel *The Devil Wears Prada* by Lauren Weisberger

District 9
Written by Neill Blomkamp and Terri Tatchell

The Diving Bell and the Butterfly
Screenplay by Ronald Harwood based on the book *The Diving Bell and the Butterfly* by Jean-Dominique Bauby

Doctor Strange
Written by Jon Spaihts and Scott Derrickson & C. Robert Cargill based on the Marvel comic *Doctor Strange* by Stan Lee and Steve Ditko

Elf
Written by David Berenbaum

Erin Brockovich
Written by Susannah Grant

Ex Machina
Written by Alex Garland

Fences
Screenplay by August Wilson based on his stage play *Fences*

The Fifth Estate
Screenplay by Josh Singer based on the books *Inside WikiLeaks* by Daniel Domscheit-Berg and *WikiLeaks* by David Leigh and Luke Harding

Flight
Written by John Gatins

Florence Foster Jenkins
Written by Nicholas Martin

The 40-Year-Old Virgin
Written by Judd Apatow & Steve Carell

The Founder
Written by Robert Siegel

Freezer Burn: The Invasion of Laxdale
Written by Blaine Hart & Barry Kloeble and Josh Miller & Grant Harvey

Frequency
Written by Toby Emmerich

Gangs of New York
Screenplay by Jay Cocks and Steven Zaillian and Kenneth Lonergan; story by Jay Cocks

Get Out
Written by Jordan Peele

Gold
Written by Patrick Massett and John Zinman

Good Night and Good Luck
Written by George Clooney and Grant Heslov

Gravity
Written by Alfonso Cuarón and Jonás Cuarón

Hacksaw Ridge
Screenplay by Robert Schenkkan and Andrew Knight

Hairspray
Screenplay by Leslie Dixon based on the screenplay *Hairspray* by John Waters based on musical play *Hairspray* by Mark O'Donnell & Thomas Meehan

Her
Written by Spike Jonze

Hidden Figures
Screenplay by Allison Schroeder and Theodore Melfi based on the book *Hidden Figures* by Margot Lee Shetterly

How the Grinch Stole Christmas
Screenplay by Jeffrey Price & Peter S. Seaman based on the book *How the Grinch Stole Christmas!* by Dr. Seuss

The Hurt Locker
Written by Mark Boal

I Am Legend
Screenplay by Mark Protosevich and Akiva Goldsman based on the novel *I Am Legend* by Richard Matheson

I, Robot
Screenplay by Jeff Vintar and Akiva Goldsman; screen story by Jeff Vintar, suggested by the book *I, Robot* by Isaac Asimov

I, Tonya
Written by Steven Rogers

The Imitation Game
Written by Graham Moore based on the book *Alan Turing: The Enigma* by Andrew Hodges

The Informant
Screenplay by Scott Z. Burns based on the book *The Informant* by Kurt Eichenwald

Inside Man
Written by Russell Gewirtz

The Judge
Screenplay by Nick Schenk and Bill Dubuque based on a story by David Dobkin & Nick Schenk

Juno
Written by Diablo Cody

Jurassic Park
Screenplay by Michael Crichton and David Koepp based on the novel *Jurassic Park* by Michael Chrichton

The King's Speech
Screenplay by David Seidler

Lars and the Real Girl
Written by Nancy Oliver

The Last Samurai
Screenplay by John Logan and Edward Zwick & Marshall Herskovitz based on a story by John Logan

Legally Blonde
Screenplay by Karen McCullah & Kirsten Smith based on the novel *Legally Blonde* by Amanda Brown

The Life of David Gale
Written by Charles Randolph

Lincoln
Screenplay by Tony Kushner based in part of the book *Team of Rivals: The Political Genius of Abraham Lincoln* by Doris Kearns Goodwin

Lion
Screenplay by Luke Davies based on the book *A Long Way Home* by Saroo Brierley

Little Miss Sunshine
Written by Michael Arndt

Marie Antoinette
Written by Sofia Coppola based on the book *Marie*

Antoinette: The Journey by Antonia Fraser

The Martian
Screenplay by Drew Goddard based on the novel *The Martian* by Andy Weir

Matchstick Men
Screenplay by Nicholas Griffin & Ted Griffin based on the book *Matchstick Men* by Eric Garcia

Milk
Written by Dustin Lance Black

Million Dollar Arm
Screenplay by Tom McCarthy

Million Dollar Baby
Screenplay by Paul Haggis based on the short story collection *Rope Burns: Stories from the Corner* by F. X. Toole

Minority Report
Screenplay by Scott Frank and Jon Cohen based on the short story "The Minority Report" by Philip K. Dick

Misson Impossible: Ghost Protocol
Written by Josh Appelbaum & André Nemec based on the television series *Mission: Impossible* created by Bruce Geller

Mission Impossible: Rogue Nation
Screenplay by Christopher McQuarrie; story by Christopher McQuarrie and Drew Pearce based on the television series created by Bruce Geller

Molly's Game
Written by Aaron Sorkin based on the book *Molly's Game* by Molly Bloom

Moneyball
Screenplay by Steven Zaillian and Aaron Sorkin based on a story by Stan Chervin and the book *Moneyball: The Art of Winning an Unfair Game* by Michael Lewis

My Big Fat Greek Wedding
Written by Nia Vardalos

Napoleon Dynamite
Written by Jared Hess and Jerusa Hess

Nightcrawler
Written by Dan Gilroy

No Country for Old Men
Screenplay by Joel Coen & Ethan Coen based on the novel *No Country for Old Men* by Cormac McCarthy

Ocean's Eleven
Screenplay by Ted Griffin based on a screenplay by Harry Brown and Charles Lederer based on a story by George Clayton Johnson and Jack Golden Russell

Passengers
Written by Jon Spaihts

The Perfect Storm
Screenplay by William D. Wittliff based on the book *The Perfect Storm* by Sebastian Junger

Phantom Thread
Written by Paul Thomas Anderson

Phone Booth
Written by Larry Cohen

Pirates of the Caribbean: The Curse of the Black Pearl
Screenplay by Ted Elliott & Terry Rossio; screen story by Ted Elliott & Terry Rossio and Stuart Beattie and Jay Wolpert

The Post
Written by Liz Hannah and Josh Singer

The Revenant
Screenplay by Mark L. Smith & Alejandro G. Iñárritu based in part on the novel *The Revenant* by Michael Punke

The Ring
Screenplay by Ehren Kruger based on the novel *Ring* by Koji Suzuki

Roman J. Israel, Esq.
Written by Dan Gilroy

Room
Screenplay by Emma Donoghue based on her novel *Room*

School of Rock
Written by Mike White

Sherlock Holmes
Screenplay by Michael Robert Johnson and Anthony Peckham and Simon Kinberg; screen story by Lionel Wigram and Michael Robert Johnson based on characters created by Arthur Conan Doyle

Shutter Island
Screenplay by Laeta Kalogridis based on the novel *Shutter Island* by Dennis Lehane

Side Effects
Written by Scott Z. Burns

Silver Linings Playbook
Screenplay by David O. Russell based on the novel *The Silver Linings Playbook* by Matthew Quick

Slumdog Millionaire
Screenplay by Simon Beaufoy based on the novel *Q & A* by Vikas Swarup

Snowden
Screenplay by Kieran Fitzgerald & Oliver Stone based on the books *The Snowden Files* by Luke Harding and *Time of the Octopus* by Anatoly Kucherena

The Social Network
Screenplay by Aaron Sorkin based on the book *The Accidental Billionaires* by Ben Mezrich

Spectre
Screenplay by John Logan and Neal Purvis & Robert Wade and Jez Butterworth; story by John Logan and Neal Purvis & Robert Wade

Spotlight
Written by Josh Singer and Tom McCarthy

Star Trek: Into Darkness
Written by Roberto Orci & Alex Kurtzman & Damon Lindelof based on the television series

Star Trek created by Gene Roddenberry

Steve Jobs
Screenplay by Aaron Sorkin based on the book *Steve Jobs* by Walter Isaacson

Still Alice
Written for the screen by Richard Glatzer & Wash Westmoreland based on the novel *Still Alice* by Lisa Genova

Team America: World Police
Written by Trey Parker & Matt Stone & Pam Brady

Thank You for Smoking
Screenplay by Jason Reitman based on the novel *Thank You for Smoking* by Christopher Buckley

The Theory of Everything
Screenplay by Anthony McCarten based on the book *Travelling to Infinity: My Life with Stephen* by Jane Hawking

Tully
Written by Diablo Cody

Up in the Air
Screenplay by Jason Reitman and Sheldon Turner based on the novel *Up in the Air* by Walter Kim

V for Vendetta
Written by Lilly Wachowski and Lana Wachowski based on the graphic novel *V for Vendetta* by Alan Moore and David Lloyd

The Walk
Screenplay by Robert
Zemeckis & Christopher
Brown based on the book *To
Reach the Clouds* by Philippe
Petit

*We Need to Talk About
Kevin*
Screenplay by Lynne Ramsay
& Rory Steward Kinnear based
on the novel *We Need to Talk
About Kevin* by Lionel Shriver

Whiplash
Written by Damien Chazelle

Whiskey Tango Foxtrot
Screenplay by Robert Carlock
based on the book *The
Taliban Shuffle: Strange Days
in Afghanistan and Pakistan* by
Kim Barker

The Wolf of Wall Street
Screenplay by Terence Winter
based on the book *The Wolf of
Wall Street* by Jordan Belfort

Zero Dark Thirty
Written by Mark Boal

Zodiac
Screenplay by James
Vanderbilt based on the book
Zodiac by Robert Graysmith

APPENDIX II
STANDARD SCREENPLAY FORMAT

While most screenwriting software will have preprogrammed formats for screenplays, teleplays and more, if you want to have a hard copy resource at hand, the long-time industry standard book is called *The Complete Guide to Standard Script Formats, Part 1* by Cole and Haag (Part II is teleplay formats). It's printed on 8.5 x 11 sized paper, so its examples are in the exact size and font as a screenplay, which is really helpful.

APPENDIX III
GLOSSARY

action: activity with intention

activity: movement or "stage business" without an underlying purpose

adaptation: a script based on an existing creative work or true story

angle: the overarching concept from which all creative decisions flow

antagonist: the protagonist's foe; usually a character but can also take other forms, such as personal demons, illness, or Mother Nature

archetypal: when a character represents universal patterns of human nature

arena: where the story is primarily situated; it could be a locale or a subculture

avant garde: French for the "vanguard" or the "advance guard"—essentially people or ideas that are ahead of their time

backstory: events that happened before the opening of the film; they need to be conveyed to the audience so they can fully understand the story

black comedy: a style of comedy where the screenwriter makes us laugh at things that would normally horrify us

bad laughs: when an audience laughs at the film and not with the film

blind alley: a narrative trap from which there's no obvious way forward (a cousin to "painted into a corner")

blockbuster: a high-budget movie featuring big stars and promoted by a huge marketing campaign

caper: a crime subgenre that involves some kind of heist

cautionary tale: a story intended to warn audiences of a certain danger

central characters: the protagonist, the antagonist, the love interest, and any other major characters who have an equal or near-equal stature or screen time to the protagonist

character: the true essence of a person (see *persona*)

character arc: the process of change a protagonist undergoes, resulting in some sort of character growth

clichés: overused genre conventions that call attention to themselves and distract from the story

climax: the final moment in the confrontation where either the protagonist or antagonist prevails

comedy: a story with a happy ending (see *tragedy*)

conflict: the outcome of opposing forces as they encounter each other

conventions: certain actions, plots, archetypes, or other elements of story that are common to particular genres

counteraction: something that's happening in a scene that either comments on or contrasts with the action, yielding irony

crisis: the biggest and most seemingly insurmountable obstacle that the protagonist faces; also called the black moment

critique: a verbal or written set of notes identifying areas for improvement in a screenplay

delayed exposition: exposition that isn't introduced until later in the story as a technique to engage the audience

deus ex machina: a Latin term that describes a weak plot point where the very thing the protagonist desperately needs suddenly and miraculously appears and is available for use

dialogue: the words spoken aloud by the characters

dominant character trait: the essence of who a character is as a person; a fundamental quality that guides the character's actions and decisions

dramatic objective: a concrete and quantifiable result the protagonist seeks (e.g., winning a championship)

ensemble: a group of central characters, each with their own subnarratives and story arcs

exposition: information the audience needs about people, places, and things so they can follow the story

false ending: a twist where the audience is led to believe the story is over, but then a final threat or twist arises

fast break: a pulse-quickening opening sequence (see *slow build*)

fatal flaw: a dominant character trait that inexorably leads the protagonist to a tragic end

first draft: the expansion from a treatment into a screenplay

flashback: a scene or sequence that jumps back in time (see *flash-forward*)

flash-forward: a scene or sequence that jumps forward in time (see *flashback*)

foreshadowing: an element that provides a subtle hint of future events and/or outcomes in a figurative, non-literal way

genre: a "type" of story, such as a mystery, romance, western, or musical

ground rules: the logic parameters of the story

Gun in the Drawer: a situation where, in order to build tension, the audience is aware of a threat while the characters are oblivious (also called the *Bear on the Beach*)

imagery: in screenplays, specific visual details that suggest the whole

inciting incident: the first complication in a story; it disrupts the protagonist

kernel: the germ of a story idea

minor characters: basic characters that serve a single specific function; they often don't exist independent of a brief relationship to the central characters

montage: a technique used to bridge time; it compresses action to move through a section of the story; shots can be out of chronological sequence or may show more than one image at a time (see *series of shots*)

multilevel: containing secondary and tertiary information

naturalism: uninterpreted reality (see *realism*)

obligatory scene: a point toward the end of Act III where the protagonist faces off with the antagonist; also called the *confrontation*

obstacles: things that stand between the protagonist and their goals and
objectives

on the nose: dialogue where characters state aloud what they're thinking
or feeling

one-dimensional: the quality of characters that are single-faceted (see
three dimensionality)

option: the legal right to exclusively control a property for a specific
period of time

organic: when an element fits naturally and easily into a scene, story, or
genre

outline: a scene by scene description of a story in bullet form

overlapping: when two or more characters talk at the same time

parenthetical: a qualifying word or words inserted in parentheses
between the character heading and the dialogue

Parking Lot Test: the informal debrief that audiences have about a film
after seeing it; if the context of the discussion is about flaws in
the film's logic or other deficient story elements, word-of-mouth
reviews will be negative

payoff: the moment a setup comes into play (see *setup*)

permission to laugh: letting the audience know as early as possible
the nature of the humor in the story, so that the audience clearly
understands what is and isn't meant to be funny

persona: how a person presents himself or herself to the world (see
character)

personal goal: something the protagonist needs to prove about
themselves, usually—but not always—through attainment of the
dramatic objective

phone call: any type of wired or wireless communication

poetry of the vernacular: idioms, vocabulary, and rhythm sourced in a
character's origins, class, and education

point of attack: where to begin a scene (see *point of departure*)

point of departure: where to end a scene (see *point of attack*)

point of view: what the writer wants to say or prove by telling the story

premise: a short phrase that captures the theme of the story; it represents the author's belief or point of view

prop: an item that a character can hold in their hand

proscenium: the arched opening that frames the stage and provides an imaginary "fourth wall" separating the audience from the actors

protagonist: the primary central character in a story

public domain: properties that are old enough that copyright has expired, leaving them available for anyone to adapt

realism: a representation of reality (see *naturalism*)

red herring: a detail that seems like it will be important, but ends up being inconsequential

resolution: the final beat of the story where the dust settles and the plot and subplots are fully resolved

rhythm: the balance between scenes that are long/short, day/night, interior/exterior, dialogue and non-dialogue and so forth

rights: the legal ability to exploit a property

rising action: in Act I, a series of conflicts and adjustments sparked by the inciting incident

road picture: a story where the protagonist must travel from point A to point B, pressured by a deadline

scene: action that takes place in one area, as defined by a lighting setup

series of shots: a technique used to bridge time; it compresses action to move through a section of the story; shots are sequential (see *montage*)

setup: a critical detail that will come into play later in the story (see *payoff*)

sitcom: short for *situation comedy*, typically a type of television series, but can also include films

situation: circumstances the characters are stuck in and can't readily escape

slow build: a movie opening that takes its time getting underway (see *fast break*)

Smoking Gun: an incriminating piece of evidence in a detective/mystery story that unequivocally confirms the guilt of the perpetrator of the crime

story: the vehicle used by the screenwriter to prove a point or share a point of view

story consultant: a professional screenplay analyst who provides written notes for a fee

subplot: secondary story lines that parallel, intersect, or contrast with the primary story line

substance: a point of view that's held by the writer

subtext: what characters are actually thinking or feeling (as opposed to what they say aloud)

superior position: when the audience has information that one or more of the characters lack

supporting characters: characters who support the central characters and who usually don't themselves undergo character growth

symbol: something that indicates, signifies, or represents an idea, object, or relationship

talking heads: static characters who exchange dialogue and don't move around

tangible stakes: the consequences that will befall the protagonist (personal) and others (external) if the protagonist fails to attain their dramatic objective/personal goal.

teaser: an opening that leaves the audience momentarily wondering what's happening or what's about to happen

time lock: some kind of deadline

time transition: a visual technique to show the passage of time

three-dimensionality: the quality of characters who are both distinct and complex

tone: the story sensibility

tragedy: a story with a sad ending (see *comedy*)

transformational: the quality of a character that causes them to catalyze change in others

treatment: a scene by scene description of a story before the inclusion of formal dialogue

twists: sudden and unexpected plot turns that, in retrospect, are completely logical

Acknowledgments

Many thanks to my friends at Brush Education: Glenn Rollans, Lauri Seidlitz and Tom Lore. I've also been extremely fortunate to have had some great mentors over my career and would specifically like to acknowledge Arthur Hiller, Fil Fraser and Dr. Charles Allard, all of whom who are no longer with us, but upon whose shoulders we stand. And finally, I'd be remiss if I didn't thank my friend Vern Oakley for coming up with a great title for this book, without which I would likely have been... you guessed it... stuck!